W0017376

WHO AM I?

Memoirs of a transformative Black Studies program

EDITED BY VANESSA GALLMAN

© 2020 Vanessa Gallman All rights reserved. No part of this publication may be repro-
duced, distributed, or transmitted in any form or by any means, including photocopying,
recording, or other electronic or mechanical methods, without the prior written permis-
sion of the publisher, except in the case of brief quotations embodied in critical reviews
and certain other noncommercial uses permitted by copyright law.

ISBN 978-1-09833-507-6

eBook 978-1-09833-508-3

ACKNOWLEDGEMENTS

This project is the brainchild of Bertha Maxwell Roddey, founding director of both the Africana Studies Department at the University of North Carolina at Charlotte and the National Council for Black Studies. After been honored by former students during a Native American-inspired "circle of appreciation," she wanted a way to showcase students from the UNCC program's early days.

Thanks to all who took the time to share their experiences. David and Jackie Sanders, Sheryl Westmoreland and Arthur Griffin Jr. provided support and outreach. Special appreciation to Andell McCoy for her diligence and the contribution of her original art for the book.

INTRODUCTION

Who am I?
Why am I here?
Where did I come from?
Where do I go from here?

These soul-searching questions formed the foundation of an innovative Black Studies program at the University of North Carolina at Charlotte, created in 1969 in the wake of political assassinations and in the midst of anti-war and Black Power protests.

At the time, UNCC was a quiet commuter college transitioning into a university; there were fewer than a dozen Black students on campus. The city of Charlotte had been spared a lot of public protest and would be considered a national model for busing after a 1971 U.S. Supreme Court decision against the local school district.

However, a December 1968 campus appearance by Stokely Carmichael, honorary prime minister of the Black Panther Party, brought race into the spotlight.

Organized by UNCC student-activist Benjamin Chavis Jr., the event created added controversy when the Black Panthers insisted that students from historically Black Johnson C. Smith University in Charlotte get seating priority over white UNCC students. In his wide-ranging talk, Carmichael denounced white oppression but also called on Blacks to take more responsibility for their own lives, according to a transcript at UNCC's J. Murrey Atkins Library.

The Dec. 18, 1968, edition of UNCC's Carolina Journal gives top display to the campus speech by a leader of the Black Panther Party. Source: ncdigital.org

"We must have an undying love for our people," he said. "We must begin to counteract the hatred that has been inculcated in our hearts by whites for hundreds of years." UNCC students decided to lobby for a university-endorsed Black Student Union (BSU), even though Chavis was then president of the Student Union Board. The student board initially denied the request. On Feb. 26, 1969, the students issued 10 demands that included recognizing the BSU, hiring Black faculty, creating a Black Studies program and recruiting more Black students.

Making any demands was risky at the time.

Gov. Bob Scott had ordered college officials to bring in police if students "threaten public order." The situation had already been tense on campus during a Feb. 7 recognition of the three protesters killed in 1968 when highway patrol officers opened fire at South Carolina State University in Orangeburg.

Benjamin Chavis Jr.   *T.J. Reddy*   *Ronald R. Caldwell*

"We took down the American flag and ran a black one up the flagpole," recalled student-activist Thomas James "T.J." Reddy in a 2017 Creative Loafing interview. "You would have thought we had committed the most heinous crime. We were surrounded by armed guards, and there were snipers on the buildings aiming rifles at us."

Later, in May, the National Guard shot up two dorms at historically Black North Carolina A&T University in Greensboro during days of violence that started over the election of a student-body president at a nearby Black high school. School officials' refusal to recognize the winner, who had championed "Black Power," led to a revolt against segregation and police oppression. One college student died, 300 people were arrested and 27 were hurt or wounded.

At UNCC, the peaceful protests were led primarily by three students: Chavis, who would later head the NAACP and organize the 1995 Million Man March; Reddy, a visual artist/poet who died in 2019 and whose work is part of the permanent collection at UNCC; and Ronald R. Caldwell, now a physician in the Asheville, N.C., area.

Reddy and Chavis would later attract international attention as political prisoners, caught up in a federal government effort to stymie Black activists across the South.

Reddy was one of the Charlotte Three, convicted in 1972 of burning a riding stable over discrimination complaints. News reports later revealed that prosecutors paid two men to testify against the trio. Their sentences were commuted by Gov. Jim Hunt in 1979.

Chavis was one of the Wilmington Ten, convicted in 1971 of arson and conspiracy in the firebombing of a grocery store. Hunt reduced their sentences in 1978; a federal appeals court ruled in 1980 that their rights had been violated; and Gov. Beverly Perdue pardoned them in 2012.

As campus protesters, however, the three were fortunate to have had an accommodating person on the other side of the negotiating table: Vice Chancellor of Student Affairs Bonnie Cone, known as "the mother of UNCC" because she had guided its transformation from Charlotte College.

Student Ronald Caldwell oversees the removal of U.S. flag on campus to replace it with a Black one on Feb. 7, 1969. Source: J. Murrey Atkins Library

"She respected what we stood for," Caldwell said in a 2005 UNCC oral history project. "She may not have really liked our approach. But it was still within the legal framework of what we could do."

Negotiations also benefitted from the tense and often-violent times. "Because of the mood of the country with the Black Panther Party and race riots developed soon after that, there was a fear element," Caldwell said. "Everybody else assumed that we were a violent organization when we weren't."

Yet even with the eventual endorsement of top university officials, it took years of diligent committee work by students and faculty to grow from one Black history course into a program that would become an accredited department by 1984. While it was trendy to set up Black Studies programs in the late 1970s, most soon ended because of lack of funds and campus support.

"It is now one of the strongest African-American, African Studies programs in the whole United States," Chavis said during a 2005 oral history. "Why? It was set up to be a permanent part of the university, not as some of those special programs where you throw a few dollars at it."

The initial hurdles included deciding exactly what Black Studies meant, and how to ensure students and the program survived on a white Southern campus. Some Black Studies Committee members worried that candidates for director were too militant in rhetoric and style.

Bertha Maxwell   *Ann C. Carver*

Eventually, Bertha Maxwell, an education professor on campus, agreed to accept the position. While some committee members worried she was too moderate, she proceeded to create a program truly radical in structure and purpose.

The program must address the whole person, Maxwell insisted. It incorporated not just strong academics and research but also the arts, community projects, encounter sessions to build coping skills — and a healthy dose of tough love. The program became a hub for the creation of political, social, cultural and fraternal groups.

A unique aspect was the Black Studies Block, a semester in which educators coordinated to teach core humanities classes, alongside discussions of the challenges and opportunities facing Blacks. Freshmen were not just educated; they were empowered with the knowledge of their history and with high expectations for success.

While the Black Studies Committee was fortunate to find faculty members who supported these goals, it also faced hostility from some professors and department-level administrators, recalled Dr. Ann Carver, the English professor who chaired the committee. An Appalachia native who had taught at historically Black and male Morehouse College, Carver would teach in the Black Studies program and, years later, create the university's Gender Studies program.

But in the early 1970s, some academics "felt there was no such thing as a Black perspective, that Black history was negligible. Many did not think there was any Black literature," she recounted in a 2018 oral history. "You had Ph.Ds. who were not only bigoted, but willfully ignorant."

Such ignorance was effectively challenged, first and foremost, by the determination and capabilities of the students — not just those who protested to create the program but those who proved the program's relevance.

They demonstrated enough self-confidence to attend a white college during a time of racial discord and social upheaval. They did so for the opportunities such an education promised. But most also understood that integration for racial progress was the mission of their generation.

This collection of memories and perspectives reveals that the students — most of them the first in their families to go to college — also knew they needed to help themselves. They benefitted from the mentorships, the teaching or simply the existence of a Black Studies program.

And the lifelong search for the answers to the fundamental "Who am I" questions have steeled the sense of purpose.

Student Benjamin Chavis Jr. speaks with Charlotte City Councilman Sandy R. Jordan March 3, 1969 during the protest for the Black Student Union. Source: J. Murrey Atkins Library

Co-founders Dr. Bertha Maxwell Roddey, left, and Dr. Mary T.
Harper, in front of the Harvey Gantt Center for African-American
Art + Culture in downtown Charlotte –Source: Ganttcenter.org

DEDICATION

Bertha Maxwell Roddey, founding director of what is now the Department of Africana Studies at the University of North Carolina at Charlotte, has been called "the mother of the Black Studies movement."

In 1975, she founded and chaired the National Council for Black Studies, which promoted the expansion of African and African-American studies, with a focus on academic excellence and social responsibility.

At least 20 U.S. universities now offer master's degrees in the field; 19 offer doctorates. UNCC offers two interdisciplinary master's degrees and a graduate certificate.

A native of Seneca, S.C., Dr. Roddey received a bachelor of arts degree from Johnson C. Smith University in North Carolina, a master's of education from the University of North Carolina at Greensboro, and a doctorate from Union Graduate School in Cincinnati.

Working for the Charlotte public school system, she started the city's first Head Start program and became the first African-American principal of a predominantly white school. She became the first Black female professor at UNCC, training middle-school teachers.

In 1969, she launched the university's Black Studies program, leading it to full department status in 1984. She retired from teaching in 1986 as the Frank Porter Graham Emeritus Professor in Africana Studies. In her honor, the university holds an annual lecture series in Africana studies.

Dr. Roddey also has been a leader in cultural, fraternal and community endeavors. From 1992-96, she served as national president of Delta Sigma Theta Sorority, which has more than 1,000 collegiate and alumni chapters internationally.

Along with her Black Studies colleague, Dr. Mary T. Harper, she founded Charlotte's Afro-American Cultural Center, now the Harvey Gantt Center for African-American Art + Culture. The center was opened in 1974, preserving an historic Black church building with help from city and university leaders. It not only provided public access to discussions and displays of Black history and culture, it gave UNCC students a base for community outreach and hands-on education.

She served on more than 50 boards and commissions; included among them was Habitat for Humanity, for which she led the process of building 350 homes in the U.S., Africa and the Caribbean.

Her most cherished awards include the Thurgood Marshall Award of Education; Order of the Long Leaf Pine awarded for service to North Carolina; the Elizabeth Catlett-Delta Legacy "Women Making a Difference" award; and the Eagle Fly Free Award from the Institute for the Advancement of Multicultural & Minority Medicine, honoring her health-education efforts as a survivor of breast cancer and brain cancer.

An extensive biography, "After the Marches: Bertha Maxwell Roddey's Educational Activism in the Desegregated South," is forthcoming from the University Press of Florida.

Her experiences "reveal the often-overlooked stories of Black women who fought against racism and sexism to help African-American students progress after the height of the Civil Rights

Movement, after the marches," said biographer Sonya Ramsey, UNCC associate professor of history and women's and gender studies.

"As a member of Delta Sigma Theta Sorority, it has been an honor to write about one of the sorority's past national presidents as a way to examine the complex dimensions of Black women's leadership," she said. "I look forward to sharing the book with her former students, colleagues, Delta sorors, and those who have yet to meet Dr. Bertha."

SECTION I

CHANGING CAMPUS CULTURE

WE COULDN'T BREATHE

By Humphrey S. Cummings

Bertha Maxwell Roddey has earned, captured and holds an important slice of history in the life cycle of UNC Charlotte. She proved to be a courageous traveler ('cause she had to be) in the making of the history of the university, the region and the nation.

As a tireless soul in motion ('cause she had to be), she pricked the consciousness of many of us at the university and in the world of academia, as she led the university — kicking and screaming most of the way — to an innovative and visionary African-American and African Studies discipline rooted in service to community.

We often hear, using the traveler's analogy, that we do our best work when we know "to stay in our lane." Bertha's lanes of travel — which include stops to fill potholes, gather like-minded workers and influence converts — is to weed out the paths to self-awareness, find the road of self-development, explore the highway of self-actualization, and journey on the expressways to self-worth.

Vision is the key to determining the destination. Innovation is the tool for determining the course of action. That makes her a most unique educator, worthy of our collective memoirs and our historical attributes — past, present and future.

One is never a "former student" when it comes to Dr. Roddey. She becomes part of your life experience and remains so throughout your life, if — to loosely paraphrase Dr. Martin Luther King Jr. — you are a drum major for improving the human condition and yourself.

I came to know her because colleagues, influencers and schoolmates directly challenged the UNCC administration, insisting that it live up to its claimed status of being a university in service to its community.

Not unlike what we see happening today, students and others of that era had the university community bear witness to soul-stirring events that could not be ignored and no longer deferred.

Some of those students included Ben Chavis, Ruth Slone, T.J. Reddy, Ronald Caldwell, Steve Browner, Sara Scott, Marva Pickett, Geraldine Dillard, Elaine Nichols, Kenneth Simmons, Dorothy Burgess, David Sanders, Ronald Swann, Sammy McGriff, Dorothy Conley, Kenneth Foster, Jackie Stevens, Laura Foxx, Octavia Walker, Mary and Spencer Singleton, Paul Hemphill, Reginald Thompson, Ben Robinson, Ben Byers, Jerry Springs, Brenda Glenn, Margo Douglas, Edward Ellis, Brenda Hogue, Norris Dae and James Cuthbertson.

Luckily, we also had community allies. Three who come to mind include Jim Grant, Phyllis Lynch and Arthur Lynch.

Our university had not listened attentively or responded effectively to our protests, grievances and demands for full equality in the university experience. A subset of students, with support of allies, came together and removed the American flag from the flagpole outside the student union building. A Black flag was hoisted in its stead. This sent a palpable, unmistakable message, a clarion call and an SOS to the university, the community and the nation.

Black students had been advocating for equality in student-life funding, and the recognition and housing of a Black Student Union. We demanded relevance and honesty — contributions of Black scholars, scientists, humanitarians in the courses taught, and for a program in Black Studies.

This symbolic act of defiance and protest — this collective "We can't breathe" moment — garnered attention on the airways and in newsprint from one end of the state to the other and beyond. It was finally settling in with administrators that simply being sympathetic in rhetoric would not placate, obfuscate, deflect, defer or deter. Only action would cement the peace.

When faculty and administrators such as William Mathis, dean of the College of Arts and Sciences, claimed that academically worthy Black scholars would not come to our university (it's too new, too raw, academically unrenowned, without big enough endowments), it gained no takers.

"Why are you here, then?" "What does that say about your scholarship?" were unanswered retorts from Black students. That left the university with but one option: Just do it.

Not to say that this meant clear sailing. What it did mean was that Dr. Roddey was recruited (maybe to placate, perhaps to delay or earnestly to bring about change). And there the paradox crystallizes.

This is where Bertha Maxwell Roddey — the unrelenting visionary, innovative bringer of worker bees, allies and converts — became and remains part of UNCC history.

That history, that legacy, that irrepressible soul in motion inspired me, helped direct me and served as a light post to me.

◊ ◊ ◊

Humphrey S. Cummings of Charlotte is an attorney in private practice. He has been a senior trial attorney and an administrative judge for the U.S. Equal Employment Opportunity Commission. After receiving a B.A. in political science with a Black Studies minor from UNCC in 1972, he earned a law degree from UNC-Chapel Hill in 1976. He has also served on the Charlotte-Mecklenburg Planning Commission and the Park and Recreation Commission.

NO MORE 'SINK OR SWIM'

By Esther Bruce

The 1970s was a time of great change. I arrived at the university as green as green can be. I grew up at the end of the Jim Crow era, and I had spent most of my education in segregated schools. Truly, when North Carolina schools desegregated, there was little to no concern about the well-being of Black students.

That was true on the campus at the University of North Carolina at Charlotte, like most other institutions. My life was changing in so many ways.

Sink or swim — that seemed to be the unstated mandate for Black students at UNCC.

The Black Studies program was born; and with its birth came a voice that not only educated students, it filled in so many gaps in the lives of underserved Black students. The program provided strong education and a place where someone knew our names and cared that we were there. The program extended a lifeline to many who needed one.

The program was in its infancy when I started at UNCC. I met some program instructors who influenced me through their dedication to truth, and the desire to enlighten and strengthen the academic, social and cultural understanding of Black students. This includes the International Festival at UNCC, where we were a part of that groundbreaking program at its inception.

Professors Bertha Maxwell Roddey, Mary Harper, Herman Thomas, Okono Oguah and Gregory Davis especially impacted and enhanced my time at UNCC. Two staff members, Claudette Cofield and Roberta Duff, were essential to the success of the program and important to the lives of students.

I am grateful to program leaders who saw a need and fought to meet it. I am a beneficiary of the program in ways that are a part of who I am today.

Esther Bruce of Charlotte retired in 2007 from a 30-year career as an educator. She also has worked as an English professor at UNCC, Johnson C. Smith University and Central Piedmont Community College in Charlotte, and at Livingstone College in Salisbury, N.C. She earned three UNCC degrees: a B.A. in French in 1975, adding a major in English in 1977, and completing an M.A. in English in 1982. She is a charter member of the Laurinburg Alumnae Chapter of Delta Sigma Theta Inc.

DEMANDS LED TO CAMPUS REBIRTH

By Paul E. Hemphill

Not written on a mountaintop or carved in stone, the students' "Ten Demands" nevertheless arrived as thunder on the campus of UNC-Charlotte. They were accompanied by lightning in the forms of sharp debates, discussions, disagreements, arguments and electric emotions.

The list of demands of obvious improvements needed on campus was the product of the Black Student Union, organized to combat (non-violently) institutionalized racism and disenfranchisement. I was elected its first president.

Rattling the false idols of white privilege and exceptionalism, the demands were hand-delivered to the chancellor and other university officers, and were posted on doors of every building and in spaces for announcements or notices. They were printed in colorful chalk on the sidewalks leading into the administration building and the student union.

Our intentions were to ensure every student knew our demands, including the need for more Black professors and for a Black Studies department.

Earlier that month, we had held a vigorous protest in front of the administration building. It was attended by about 15 Black UNCC students and about 20 students from historically Black Johnson C. Smith University and an unruly crowd of mostly white students. The campus police were reinforced by the Mecklenburg County Police Department. Local news media were also present.

Ronnie Caldwell went to the flagpole and took down Old Glory and raised a black flag that flew throughout our demonstration. It was a very intense and interesting day.

The administration later agreed to most of our demands, which birthed a new chapter in education at UNCC. It also brought to us a wonderful, kind and intelligent professor who was a fierce advocate for Black students.

Dr. Bertha Maxwell Roddey is the mother of the UNCC Black Studies program, the first such department at a predominantly majority U.S. university. Arguably, she is the mother of all Black Studies, for UNCC offered a template for other universities.

"Mother Bertha," as she known to many of her students, is a mentor and a friend. She unknowingly made it possible for me to meet the woman who would become my wife, Pamela Hart Hemphill, when she invited me to speak to her class on civil rights in 1977.

Pam and I cherish and respect Mother Bertha and will always hold to her teachings for a better world. We, along with her other students, will always be there for her and cherish the personal guidance intellectually and collectively.

◊ ◊ ◊

The Rev. Paul E. Hemphill Esq. of Charlotte retired from a 33-year law career and is now an associate minister at New St. John Missionary Baptist Church. He graduated from UNCC in 1972 with a B.A. in history and minor in English literature and education. He earned a law degree from North Carolina Central University in 1975. He worked for Legal Services and in private practice before attending Southern Evangelical Seminary in Charlotte to receive a master of divinity degree. A charter member of Zeta Delta Chapter of Kappa Alpha Psi, he is now an active life member.

FINALLY, I BELONGED

By Vernetta Conley Foxx

During my freshman year at UNCC, the Black Studies Block did not exist, so we had to take the same classes as all students did. The classes were very difficult; there was a big difference from my high school classes in Morganton, a small town.

During my second year, the new freshman did enroll in The Block courses and were so happy and felt so smart because their grades and GPAs were great. I did enroll in some Black Studies courses, and the experience was wonderful.

I felt like someone liked me on campus. I felt like it was my school and that the instructors were real people. The classes afforded you an opportunity to talk, listen and collaborate; and learning was taking place at the same time.

The math classes I took were taught mostly by men who were just being "men who loved math" whether you did or not. There were some whom you could talk to. But in most classes, you did not talk; you listened, solved problems and took notes.

One highlight of the Black Studies program was participating in a talent event. Several of my friends and I performed as The Pointer Sisters singing "Yes We Can Can."

◊ ◊ ◊

Vernetta Conley Foxx of Charlotte has been a high-school math teacher for 27 years at Victory Christian Center School, where she has received various honors for service and teaching excellence. She earlier taught at West Charlotte High School and was a computer programmer for 11 years at Barclays American Corp. She earned a B.A. in math from UNCC in 1978. She has been a leader in a summer camp for low-income students, and held many leadership roles in Victory Christian Church.

WEALTH OF EXPERIENCES

By Charles L. Webber

I entered UNCC as a freshman in fall 1970. Some of my early experiences on campus included participating on the freshman basketball team and joining Kappa Alpha Psi Fraternity. While an undergraduate, I enrolled in Black Experience I and II with Dr. Bertha Maxwell and an adjunct instructor whose name fails me at the moment.

I have very fond remembrances of my time with the Black gospel choir, as well as being involved to a lesser degree with the Black Student Union.

While some of the details are fuzzy, I recall participating musically in an event that was part of Dr. Maxwell's doctoral degree requirements. During my time on campus, social activism was alive and well as students Ben Chavis of the Wilmington Ten and T.J. Reddy of the Charlotte Three were making their imprints on the local and national scenes.

It was a time of racial, social and gender pandemics, police brutality, campus student unrest and protest over civil rights and the Vietnam War. Interestingly, some of the same social and political issues prevalent then are confronting our nation now.

◊ ◊ ◊

Charles L. Webber, of Shelby, N.C., is a city councilman and pastor of Mount Olive Baptist Church in Kings Mountain, N.C. He retired in 2008 after a 33-year career in human resources for local governments. From UNCC, he earned a degree in sociology with a minor in political science in 1974 and a master's in public administration in 1998. With a master of divinity degree from Gardner-Webb University, he is now a candidate for a doctorate there. He also spent 20 years in the U.S. Army Reserves and taught social studies in Cleveland County schools.

GAINED INDIRECT BENEFITS

By Dorothy Faye Conley

Because of scheduling conflicts, I was an indirect beneficiary of the Black Studies program. It was being formed in 1969 during my second year at UNCC. During that time, there was a strong bond among the majority of Black students, including those who commuted, because there were so few of us.

It was so refreshing to have the prowess of an educator, so focused on our Blackness, grace the campus. I suspect I was able to get to know Dr. Bertha Maxwell because there were so few Black students. I value the many conversations I had with her, even after I graduated.

While I did not take any classes, I was able to participate in any available non-classroom activities that my schedule would allow. I also benefitted from other students' sharing that helped broaden the knowledge of who I was and could be as a young, gifted and Black woman.

◊ ◊ ◊

Dorothy Faye Conley, of Gaithersburg, Md., retired as a church administrator in 2017 and is completing an eight-year term as president of the Second Episcopal District Women's Missionary Society of the African Methodist Episcopal Church. She earned a B.A. in mathematics, minoring in philosophy, from UNCC in 1972. She also had a technical career at IBM and worked as director of information technology at Black Entertainment Television.

FOUND: A CAMPUS HOME

By Maudine McFadden Cornish

T he Black Studies program, under the leadership of Dr.
Bertha Maxwell Roddey, was like being in your home away
from home.

When I reminisce about my days at UNCC, my images and
thoughts go directly to my traumatic experiences of being the fifth
Black student to graduate from the B.S. in nursing program. For a
nursing student, there was rarely any time to experience anything
except to delve immensely into the nursing curriculum.

The Black Studies office as my one special place to escape to,
and where I received the much-needed encouragement and support
to develop the perseverance and strength to become a conqueror,
with the characteristics and qualities of a successful leader.

Dr. Roddey incorporated in the program several characteristics and qualities that have been the foundation for me and many
other students to become the well-accomplished human beings we

are today. She instilled in us integrity, the ability to delegate, communication, self-awareness, gratitude, learning agility, empathy, courage, respect and spiritual awareness.

I sincerely thank Dr. Roddey and all the professors and staff for the great impact they have had on my life and so many other African-Americans.

◊ ◊ ◊

Maudine McFadden Cornish, of Lanham, Md., retired after a 42-year career as a nurse at Howard University Hospital in Washington, D.C., most recently in case management. She received her B.S. in nursing from UNCC in 1976 and an M.A. in mental health and gerontology from the University of the District of Columbia in 1983.

GROUNDBREAKING EXPERIENCES

By Spencer Singleton

During the time I attended UNCC, I was afforded ample opportunities to take part in groundbreaking developments. Chief among these were the creation of the Black Student Union and the program that would become the Department of Africana Studies, both of which were established in 1969.

The BSU was created out of necessity. The fledgling population of Black students at the university desired a body that would address their unique needs and concerns. The 1972 National Black Political Convention in Gary, Ind., had a contingency of UNCC students in attendance, thanks to efforts of Dr. Bertha Maxwell of the Black Studies program, Vice Chancellor Bonnie Cone and the BSU.

Kappa Alpha Psi Fraternity, Zeta Delta Chapter, has the distinction of being the first national Greek-lettered fraternity at UNCC.

I had the honor of being on that charter line in spring 1970. Also, during the early years of the sports programs, I played trumpet with the inaugural Pep Band, which had 10 members at the time.

Dec. 2, 1972, was a very special day: Mary Simpson, a UNCC alumnus, and I were married. We held our wedding reception in the student union, now the Cone Center.

Spencer Singleton of Charlotte is a retired major in the U.S. Air Force who taught social studies in public schools for 17 years before retiring in 2011. He earned a B.A. in history and a teacher certification in secondary education from UNCC, and an M.A. in management from Webster University while in the military. Currently an instructor for 14 school chess clubs, he and his wife also run a nonprofit that hosts Bible studies and provides materials for them.

NAVIGATING REAL LIFE

By Mary Simpson Singleton

For me, UNCC was an experience in "real-world existence." My interactions with Caucasians had been limited to one year in high school. I must admit to a sheltered life. My mother made every attempt to protect her enormous brood from the ravages of poverty and racism. I guess one might say I did a lot of growing up as a 49er.

I had known Dr. Roddey as a child, around third grade, but had not seen her since elementary school. We can try to avoid overused terminology, but it's futile to try to describe the role she played in my life as anything less than "Queen Mother."

She helped us to navigate prejudice, rejection and insecurities. She was an encourager, coach, confidant and mother confessor.

When Spencer and I reignited our childhood romance while at UNCC and decided to marry, she was our adviser. She asked us a question that I remember to this day: "What do you think your first argument will be about?"

I won't tell the answer, but she was right.

The Black Student Union was another big part of the learning puzzle. Such passion, such intellect, such wisdom. Yes, we were young and foolish, but united in righteous endeavor.

The most beautiful thing I remember about the trips, marches, even a trip to the first National Black Political Convention in Gary, Ind., was the support of Vice Chancellor Bonnie Cone. She was a wonder and a great friend to the BSU.

I discovered my life's work, teaching, at UNCC. I can say without reservation, my alma mater prepared and equipped me for success.

Mary Simpson Singleton of Charlotte worked as a special-education teacher in four states and in Italy on local and university levels, as well as in adult instruction and counseling. In addition to a receiving a bachelor's in political science and a secondary teaching certificate from UNCC in 1974, she earned a master of education degree from Wright State University in Dayton, Ohio.

KEY FOCUS: GIVING TO OTHERS

By Barbara Roseboro Myers

My journey at UNC Charlotte was more than I ever could have imagined the day I stepped on campus. Coming from a small town at the foothills of the mountains in western North Carolina, I was in awe at the buildings, the people and the city.

Even though my closest friends, Faye and Vernetta Conley, were at UNCC, I was experiencing a high level of anxiety and fear of the unknown. There was the process of getting to know roommates, finding classes, making sure finances were in place, as well as getting to know new people, which for me was a task as I was rather shy. I had never been away from the comfort and support of home and family.

However, Faye and Vernetta were the best in helping me become familiar with day-to-day activities, and the individuals in the Black Studies Department were supportive as well.

But my greatest comfort came when I met Bertha Maxwell (affectionately called "Bertha"), whose mannerism and comforting spirit reminded me so much of my mother. It was this woman of such high character that embraced this little mountain girl and helped her to see the value in learning all you can, staying focused and giving of yourself for the betterment of others.

You see, the Black Studies professors and staff recognized their high calling and the importance of teaching us to be mindful of who we were and our responsibility for the welfare of our fellow man. As a result of my experiences at UNCC, I find myself very much involved in my community.

I am grateful to soror Bertha Maxwell Roddey for helping me to realize my potential. Even after college, she came to support me at local chapter events as our speaker. Such a woman.

Barbara Roseboro Myers, of Morganton, N.C., was the first African-American director of the social work program at Broughton Hospital, a state psychiatric hospital. Recipient of the Order of the Long Leaf Pine and the Caswell Award for dedication and excellence, she will retire with more than 47 years of state service. She is president of the Burke County branch of the NAACP and secretary/treasurer of Blue Ridge Community Action board of directors. After a B.A. in sociology and anthropology from UNCC in 1973, she earned a master of social work degree from UNC-Chapel Hill in 1981. She was a charter member of both the UNCC chapter and the Hickory Alumnae Chapter of Delta Sigma Theta Sorority.

READIED FOR CORPORATE LIFE

By Robyn Massey

C oming to UNC Charlotte was a questionable decision, at least in my Mom's mind. I grew up in the Raleigh area, and my family expected I would attend a great school there. I was accepted early into both UNC-Chapel Hill and North Carolina State.

In the 1970s, UNCC was a young university, so it did not have a strong reputation. Before I made my decision, I spoke to several church members and high-school friends who attended there. They told me that I should consider attending, as the classes were smaller and the faculty readily accessible. Let's just say that when I arrived on campus in the fall of 1977, my family was not thrilled.

I became a member of the largest Black class to date at the university and quickly bonded with my classmates. But as a math major, I rarely had classes with Black students other than freshman English with Dr. Mary Harper and religious studies with Dr. Herman Thomas.

Taking classes with those professors enriched my experience. They were both demanding, but you knew they had your best interests at heart by pushing to make sure you were adequately prepared for the real world.

During my junior and senior years, I took a couple of Black Studies courses. Both courses became critical in framing how I retained my identity through my professional career. My experience as the only person of color in many classes provided a realistic glimpse of my future. Those classes, particularly one I took under George Goodman, provided perspective of how to integrate into corporate America while not losing my own identify.

Although I was always one of the few or the only person of color in my high-school classes, there was lunch or some activity daily where I could be with my peeps. My time at UNCC clarified that, in the real world and because of my chosen profession, code switching would become a way of life.

Robyn Massey of Charlotte is a retired IBM project executive whose career including consulting on talent and technology in Durban, South Africa. After receiving her bachelor's in mathematics from UNCC, she earned an MBA from Wake Forest University. President of the UNCC Alumni Board from 2008-2010, she received the Distinguished Alumni Award in 2016.

EMBOLDENED WITH PRIDE

By Brenda Steadman

W hen I entered UNCC in August 1970, I was Brenda Kay Glenn. I left in 1974 known as "East Bend."

During those four years, I was perceived as someone who came from a small town to the big city. I just wanted to attend college. I came to the campus sight unseen and had never been to Charlotte.

So, why UNCC? Oh, it was the scholarship money.

My dream was to attend Livingstone College. I often wonder how my life might have been different, if only … But I will not live thinking that way. UNCC made me who I am today.

Black Studies professors Ann Carver and Mary Harper exposed me to literature that gave me a sense of who I was and who I could be. Reading "Native Son" and "The Fire Next Time" was like breathing the fresh air of a cool morning in East Bend, N.C.

I felt emboldened to let people know that "Yes, I am from East Bend, N.C. and proud of it." I wear that name with pride.

Thank you, Dr. Carver and Dr. Harper. And a special thank you to Roberta Duff who always greeted me warmly as I entered the Black Studies office.

For those who know me as East Bend, always remember that we have perceptions of people based on what we know at that time. I refuse to lament about the hurt I felt during that time in my life.

Now, that time continually blesses me with the relationships I built and shows me how to bless others. Oh, what a life I have been given because of His grace and peace. The Black Studies Department, under the leadership of Dr. Bertha Maxwell Roddey, was my safe haven. Thank you, "Mother Bertha."

◊ ◊ ◊

Brenda Steadman, of Greensboro, N.C., retired as a teacher in Guilford County Schools in 2015. She earned her B.A. in sociology from UNCC in 1974 and a master's in education at the University of North Carolina in Greensboro in 1986. In 2015, the governor's office honored her with The Order of the Long Leaf Pine for service to the state.

SUPPORT FOR STUDENTS

By Marva Wiley

M any of the African-American students at UNCC gathered in
the student union between classes and during their lunch
breaks to support one another, sing and enjoy the fellowship.
Eventually, the Black Student Union was formed, where concerns
were voiced about the state of African-American students on
campus.

As a result, a committee of students and professors was formed
to look closer at the situation and decide what might be done to
make a difference on campus. I served on that committee.

One of the decisions was to develop a Black Studies program.
After many long hours of discussion and planning, Dr. Bertha
Maxwell Roddey was chosen to develop and head the program. Many students who visited the program's offices and attended
its classes received the support and encouragement they needed to
pursue their goals.

In addition to serving on the committee, I attended some Black Studies classes and was one of the first African-Americans to graduate from UNCC's nursing program.

Marva (Pickett) Wiley of Charlotte retired in 2017 after 45 years as a registered nurse in various fields that included operating room nurse, school nurse, supervisor of an HIV case management program and supervisor of a home-visiting case management program. She earned a B.S. degree in nursing from UNCC in 1972 and a master of public health degree in nursing from UNC-Chapel Hill in 1980.

WORTH CHEERING ABOUT

By Annette Johnson Pearce

B ertha Maxwell was the epitome of Blackness at UNCC and a mother to all. She resonated love and the Black experience, and pushed us all for success on a campus where we were outnumbered. Thank you, Bertha, for showing us the way.

I had many rewarding opportunities at UNCC. I played women's basketball, sang with the Children of the Sun choir and was a member of the Black Student Union. I joined three others — Emma Gillespie, Barbara Mahan and Cynthia Bennett — to charter the Kappa Kappa Chapter of Alpha Kappa Alpha Sorority on March 18, 1976.

Also, Emma Gillespie and I were on the cheerleading team in 1973 and 1974. We followed the university's first two Black cheerleaders, Dot Burgess and Wietta Knight.

It was a great experience because the majority of the men's team were Black males, including Robert Earl Blue, Sheldon Shipman, Norris Dae, Stanley Graham, Don Pearce and Jon Heath.

We were not given the freedom to change the cheers or add any "soul" to the routines, and the band was all-white. But being able to represent us off the court was the mission.

Annette Johnson Pearce, of Hampton, Ga., retired as senior consultant for G.A. Wright Inc. marketing firm and is the widow of UNCC graduate Donald W. Pearce. She earned a B.A. in business administration from UNCC and an MBA in project management from DeVry University. She served as president of the Atlanta chapter of the National Association of Securities Professionals and as treasurer of the YWCA of Greater Atlanta. She currently serves as treasurer of her homeowners' association.

OPPORTUNITIES DELAYED

By Vanessa Moser Heggins

While at UNCC, I lived in Sanford Hall on the 11th floor. In fall 1971, I was chosen to be on the JV cheerleading squad. That was the best thing I can remember about that year. I also was a member of the gospel choir. That was fun, too.

When I returned for my sophomore year, I found out I was pregnant with my first child. I finished that semester but did not return to UNCC to continue my education until 1995.

It has been a been a pleasure to be a 49er. I recognize UNCC as my college every time I come in contact with a person who graduated from there. I am really disappointed I did not stay in contact with students from UNCC. I thank Andell McCoy, my sophomore-year roommate, for finding me and letting me know about this project.

I didn't have much to do with the Black Studies Department, but I remember Bertha Maxwell as a very strong voice and presence on campus. I send prayers that God will continue to bless her and give her the health and strength to do his will.

Vanessa Moser Heggins, of China Grove, N.C., retired in 2015 from teaching first- and second-graders in the Rowan-Salisbury School System and continues to work as a substitute teacher. After attending UNCC for three semesters in the early 1970s, she returned to complete a B.A. in elementary education in 1998. She has been active in churches her husband pastored in Charlotte and Salisbury, working with youth choirs, praise dance teams and ushers.

HELPED BUILD COMMUNITY

By Claudia Jordan

T he UNC Charlotte Black Studies program was an affirming and challenging experience. It is an understatement to say I was a naive freshman, but the environment at UNCC allowed me to flourish. It was challenging because it stretched my ideas of the world and my surroundings, and how I would fit in the world.

Students Edward Ellis and Wyman Anderson challenged me to think in broader terms and frankly appreciated my Blackness.

Our Black Student Union was active; we had heated, honest discussions about politics in Charlotte, Wilmington and the world. True to form, we had those on the left and the right; but we were a family. "Family" is the way I would describe most of my experience at UNCC.

It certainly enhanced my duty to our community. Growing up on the farm as sharecroppers, I learned early the value of the community and the support it gives. UNCC became the farm, and the students became my community.

The early students — David and Jackie Sanders, Barbara Roseboro, East Bend, Winnie McNeely, Fish, Big Dot and Brenda Hogue — were some of my mentors, big brothers and sisters. They taught me how to play bid whist and how to succeed on a campus that was at times unwelcoming.

We had protests and marched. We were part of, I hope, a change. And that attitude — a willingness to try to make a difference — has remained part of me.

Dr. Bertha Maxwell Roddey and Dr. Herman Thomas were hosts to many conferences and meetings where their guidance proved invaluable. Dr. Roddey continues to be a mentor and friend.

Claudia Jordan of Denver, Colo., was the first African-American woman appointed to the Denver County Court bench in 1994. After her 1975 graduation from UNCC, she earned a degree from the University of Colorado School of Law, then worked as a public defender and in private practice before her appointment to the bench by Mayor Wellington Webb. When the judge retired, Mayor Michael Hancock proclaimed Sept. 30, 2014, "Claudia Jordan Day."

LAUNCHING PAD

By Emma Allen

D uring the time I was a student 1979, we were very much the
minority on campus. It was wonderful to have the African-
American and African Studies Department and Dr. Bertha Roddey
as a safe haven and a home away from home.

It was the gathering place for, I think, all of the minority students on campus. I have no doubt that she intentionally created a
landing spot and launching pad to ensure our success.

◊ ◊ ◊

*Emma Allen of Charlotte is an owner/agent with State Farm
Insurance. After receiving a B.A. in business administration from
UNCC in 1984, she worked in banking, including as a senior vice
president of Wachovia Bank. Recipient of a UNCC Distinguished
Alumni Award in 2018, she serves on the Mecklenburg Zoning Board
of Adjustment.*

FINDING MY VOICE

By Linda Ross Brown

In 1971, I transferred to UNCC from Sacred Heart College my sophomore year and continued as a music major. The three years of undergraduate studies at UNCC allowed me to develop essential music skills, formulate lasting relationships and experience various unique opportunities.

I was co-founder and accompanist of the first UNCC gospel choir. The choir sang inspirational and soul-stirring music, but it also gave members and student observers opportunities to enjoy and bond with one another.

I came from a family of four siblings in Kings Mountain, N.C. However, at UNCC my family increased to where I was one of 13 sisters. I pledged Delta Sigma Theta and became a member of the charter chapter, Iota Rho, in December 1972. Our adviser was none other than the visionary, intellectual and humble Dr. Bertha Maxwell Roddey, director of the Black Studies program.

I never told Dr. Roddey how much I admired her, her professionalism and the way she respected and treated the 13 undergraduate women with dignity. I was too shy to say it then. But now, without reservation, I can say I am grateful to her for being a wonderful adviser and role model — not just for the Deltas but for all African-Americans who knew her.

Linda Ross Brown, of Pittsburgh, Pa., was a music teacher and administrator in Pittsburgh Public Schools for 33 years. She and husband, the Rev. James Brown, founded Mercy Acts International, which provides humanitarian aid in Africa, Haiti and the U.S. After graduating from UNCC in 1974, she earned M.A. degrees in music education and in education from Duquesne University in Pittsburgh. A high-school choral ensemble under her direction, accompanied by renowned cellist Yo-Yo Ma, performed one of Brown's compositions for First Lady Michelle Obama at the 2009 G20 Summit. Her 2015 CD, "Bread of Heaven," was nominated for Rhythm of Gospel Awards in five categories.

SECTION II

BUILDING ON 'THE BLOCK'

TEACHING AHEAD OF ITS TIME

By Gregory Davis

I didn't start learning to read or write until I was 12 years old, when I was allowed to attend the newly desegregated Governor Morehead School for the Blind. I got my GED and went to community college, where one administrator assumed that educating me was a waste of time because lack of sight apparently meant I was retarded.

I have spent my life proving that wrong.

I first met Dr. Maxwell Roddey during summer 1974 while attending a leadership conference at UNC Charlotte for student-government presidents. She and Dr. Herman Thomas persuaded me to finish my last two years of undergraduate work there.

I enrolled in Dr. Roddey's class, Introduction to Black Studies. By the time the semester ended, I realized there were three distinct sides of her.

The first was so persuasive she could make a person purchase a gallon of ice water at the North Pole. The second was an activist, protesting alongside Stokely Carmichael during the Mississippi Freedom Summer when he introduced the idea of "Black Power." The third was the woman of conviction whose mission was to expand the minds of students, faculty and administrators.

All three personalities combined to advocate for, and ultimately obtain, a degree-granting department for African-American and African Studies.

I graduated from UNCC and went on to divinity school. However, I returned the summer of 1978 to teach the Introductory to Black Studies course. In 1979, I graduated from Duke Divinity School with an advanced degree in religious studies, a wife and daughter — but no job.

I learned about a new position in the African-American and African Studies Department to teach courses and advise freshmen. After having been turned down for many other teaching positions and not being able to be hired as a pastor, I gladly accepted the offer. I was by far the best candidate, Dr. Roddey said, because I was a product of the original Black Studies program and had recently taught a course in the new department.

She took a chance on me. If that had not happened, I don't know what I would have done.

In my new job, I was responsible for the freshmen pursuing degrees in the department, which included four phases of course-work. During the freshman year, students had to answer the question "Who am I?" In the sophomore year, they had to answer the question "Where did I come from?" In the junior year, students had to answer "Why am I here?" In the senior year, the question was "Where do I go from here?"

Students who participated in the first phase had to take a group of core classes call "The Block." These courses included Black studies, English, math, a social science and a natural science. I taught the introductory course and required students to complete an in-class group presentation on some aspect of the Black existence.

The class of about 50 students self-selected to work in groups ranging in sizes from four to six. At the end of the semester, groups made presentations for which they were evaluated not only on content, but also on presentation skills.

I also required a community project. Students had to visit an organization that met the needs of the Black community and learn what skills were necessary for employment.

We did not know it at the time, but what we were asking students to do and how we tasked students to learn was revolutionary.

It wasn't until the turn of the century in 2000 that the university started to use for the general student population some of the teaching and educational requirements Dr. Roddey had pioneered decades prior.

The university calls them "learning communities." But their goal was to create the same kind of comprehensive, hands-on curriculum that had been infused within the African-American and African Studies Department from its beginning.

The Rev. Dr. Gregory Davis of Charlotte retired in 2008 as UNCC's director of Minority Academic Services and retired in 2017 as pastor of Bellefonte Presbyterian Church in Harrisburg, N.C., after 37 years. After graduating from UNCC with a B.A. in religious studies in 1976, he earned an M.A. from Duke Divinity School and a Ph.D. from Union Institute in Ohio. Inducted into the UNCC Hall of Fame in 2006 and named a Distinguished Alumni in 2012, he has set up a scholarship for students in need.

BLACK POWER REALIZED

By Andell McCoy

From first through fifth grades, I attended an all-Black school in my rural hometown. In sixth grade, I — along with my fourth-grade brother, first-grade sister and three other children from three different families — opted to integrate the town's white elementary school.

I was challenged by racial slurs, was the last chosen for P.E. teams, had a chair pulled from under me while the teacher was out of the room and was isolated at lunch tables. Upon graduation, I and three other Black girls were cited as a credit to the school for our resilience, as well as our personal and academic successes.

The year I entered 9th grade, all county schools fully integrated. Because I knew all the Black and all the white students, I was positioned to be a leader. I loved high school, however I was excited about getting out of Mt. Gilead and to college.

My first days at UNCC were wonderful. It was my first time away from home for more than a few weeks, and there were friendly upperclassmen Black girls on the fourth floor of Sanford Hall. We bonded quickly, sharing study, common interests and goals, meals, adventures and so much laughter. Some remain life-long friends.

I registered for the first Black Studies Block, a class of 12 to 15 smart and enthusiastic Black students from all over the state. They spoke up and stood out, each very much an individual. We were immersed in Black history, which was absent from most of my earlier scholastic materials. Our teachers were addressed on a first-name basis.

Beverly Ford introduced us to the psychology of Black people, Franz Fanon and Kenneth Clark. David Frye spoke of systemic racism, inequity and calls for social justice. We studied the revolutionary thinking of Marcus Garvey and Haile Selassie, along with Malcolm X, Martin Luther King Jr. and Angela Davis. Mary Harper and Ann Carver exposed us to Black literature, including works by James Baldwin, Richard Wright, Nikki Giovanni, Amiri Baraka and Zora Neale Hurston.

We read, we listened, spoke and wrote. We agreed, and agreed to disagree, passionately. We grew through one another's eyes. These experiences and the historical significance of Blackness, taught in a way I had not experienced before, enhanced my creative ability to express through poetry.

Prior to college, I knew about Black power, commitment and responsibility, mostly through older people in my home, church and community. I had seldom experienced this solidarity with peers. In school, I was most often in the minority. The Block offered the chance to be in the majority again.

Program director Bertha Maxwell was a tough, smart and powerful woman, with sharp edges and fire. A no-nonsense leader with a big voice and an even bigger laugh. She met us where we were, with questions "Who am I? Where do I come from? Where am I going?" She challenged us, strengthening our best parts and holding us accountable for doing what was necessary to succeed in our classes and in life.

Mother hen, Big Bird, counselor, comedian and cheerleader —
Bertha spoke truth to power, confronted conflict head-on and was
determined to get what she wanted from us and the university. She
worked diligently to support our efforts to find voice and equitable
opportunity on the UNCC campus.

*Andell McCoy, of Mt. Gilead, N.C., is a poet, artist, council facil-
itator and teacher who retired from Stanly Community College
in Albemarle, N.C. She also taught at Crosswords School and The
Archer School for Girls in California and worked in mental-health
settings. While at UNCC, she pledged Delta Sigma Theta and later
earned a B.A. in radio, TV and motion pictures from UNC-Chapel
Hill and a M.A. in psychology from Phillips Graduate University. A
UCLA Writing Project fellow, she serves on the board of the Center
for Faith and the Arts in Salisbury, N.C. Her abstract paintings have
been exhibited at Falling Rivers Gallery, the Elegba Folklore Society's
gallery, ClearWater Arts Center & Studios, and the McColl Center for
Art + Innovation.*

LEARNING OUR FULL TRUTH

By Melvin Watkins

W hat an honor to be a part of the University of North Carolina Charlotte history. It was also an honor to have experienced the courses in the Department of Africana Studies, formerly known as the Black Studies Department.

I was invited to UNCC's campus on a basketball scholarship in 1973. It was not far from my home of Reidsville, N.C. Though the college experience was a significant transition for me, I certainly had a wonderful group of coaches and teammates who supported my well-being. But the academic rigor was intimidating, especially while balancing an athletic career.

While searching through courses, I stumbled upon the Black Studies Department. The coursework was immediately familiar in many ways. I soon had the opportunity to meet the professors: Dr. Bertha Maxwell, Dr. Herman Thomas and Dr. Greg Davis. My life and my academic experience were deeply impacted by my experience with these professors and their courses.

Dr. Maxwell led the program with conviction. She strongly believed that we had not been taught our full history in primary and secondary school, and she was determined to broaden our horizon. She was the first teacher who taught me that Black history was much richer than slavery. She and her colleagues poured the full truth into our minds, making sure we understood that we were standing on the shoulders of greatness and that much was expected of us.

My life and my success as a student-athlete can absolutely be attributed to the coursework and the affirming relationships developed between students and professors through the department.

I wish all students had been given the opportunity to be a part of it. UNCC was certainly on the cutting edge by having a program such as this available to students in the 1970s. I am thankful to the forward-thinking administration.

I graduated in 1977 with a B.S. in economics, the year our basketball team was in the Final Four of the NCAA Men's Basketball Tournament. It was a very memorable year for me.

Though as I look back, I can say for sure that my academic achievements sprouted from the Black Studies Department. It was there I learned the true meaning of "good trouble."

Melvin Watkins, of Springdale, Ark., has been coaching basketball for 42 years, including 20 years at UNCC as an assistant, associate and head coach. He has been the head coach at Texas A&M University and coached at the University of Missouri and the University of Arkansas. His honors include Conference USA Coach of the Year in 1997 while at UNCC and Rivals.com's Top Assistant Coach in 2009 and 2010. At UNCC, he was All-Conference point guard from 1973-77, and led the team to its only Final Four appearance. His jersey number, 32, was retired, and he was drafted by the Buffalo Braves in the fourth round of the NBA Draft.

EMBRACING CAMPUS LIFE

By Debbie Springs Woodson

I have many fond memories of the UNCC campus life, the Black Studies Block, the Black Studies professors and other campus events. I took the required freshman courses in the Block and did fairly well for a freshman getting used to college life.

The professors were tough, but they were preparing us for what we were to encounter when we would be taking courses with other professors in our majors. They prepared us well. They also encouraged us to be open to groups and opportunities offered on campus. I became active in a Bible study group, was president of the junior class and a residence advisor, and was inducted into the Society of 49 honor society.

However, my favorite activity was singing in the Black gospel choir called Children of the Sun. I participated in the choir from

1973 until 1977. Ivan, a musician living in Charlotte, was the director and pianist. The choir would sing at churches and for events on and off campus. We were well received. Ivan was just as tough on us as the Black Studies professors.

I enjoyed singing with the group and socializing with the other students so very much. Who can forget the fantastic sounds of the Children of the Sun gospel choir?

Thank you, Bertha Maxwell, Mary Harper, Herman Thomas and other Black Studies professors for everything you did for students and the university.

Debbie Springs Woodson, of Greenville, N.C., retired in 2014 from Pitt County Schools after 36 years of teaching and counseling, and now works part-time as a student-services specialist. Her career also included work in schools in Charlotte and Winston-Salem. At UNCC, she earned a B.A. in history with a concentration in early childhood education in 1977 and as a master's in human development in learning with a concentration in elementary counseling in 1982. She is on the board of Churches Outreach Network and on the application committee for Brody School of Medicine at East Carolina University. Her husband, Mark, also graduated from UNCC in 1977, earning degrees in engineering and religious studies.

SURVIVING CULTURE SHOCK

By Lonnie T. Stinson

As the son of an Air Force noncommissioned officer, I frequently moved from one location to another. From elementary schools in Columbus, Ohio, to middle schools in Mountain Home, Idaho, and even Kubasaki Junior High School in Okinawa, Japan, I was consistently surrounded by others who didn't look like me.

However, as "military brats," we never really thought or talked about it. Our dads, and sometimes moms, all wore the same uniforms, and we all wore the same style clothes from the base Exchange store. We even acquired the same generic style of speaking.

It wasn't until our family went to North Carolina and Alabama to visit relatives that I was awakened to the painful reality that we were different.

There were "white" cabs, and "white" water fountains. There were special back doors, side doors and even stairs for "colored" to enter. There were places we couldn't eat and others where we couldn't even sit.

Growing up in a multicultural and multiracial environment had prepared me to live in harmony with everyone. However, it had not prepared me for the hurtful reality of the world outside of the military.

The Black Studies program at UNCC was a lifesaver. Dr. Bertha Maxwell Roddey and her professional staff were heaven-sent.

They taught us our history. They instilled into each of us a sense of pride that the world was trying to suppress. They enlightened us to the Black experience and deepened our awareness of Black expressions.

We studied Lerone Bennett Jr.'s "Before the Mayflower" and listened to the poetic words of Nikki Giovanni. We were taught about the injustice toward the Wilmington Ten, the struggles of Angela Davis, the determination of Rosa Parks, the resolve of Malcolm X, and the dreams of the Rev. Dr. Martin Luther King Jr.

We were inspired, encouraged, mentored and challenged.

One of those challenges came from a very professional and caring English teacher, Dr. Mary T. Harper. She challenged me to do better. Unfortunately, I didn't respond appropriately at the time, and it was later reflected in my course grade.

The next year, I followed in my father's footsteps and joined the military. While serving at Fort Jackson, S.C., I enrolled in another English 102 course at the University of South Carolina. I served in uniform during the day and attended school at night. I applied myself and worked hard (like Dr. Harper taught us) and achieved an "A" in the course.

Later, while on leave from the military, I drove from Fort Jackson to UNCC to surprise and visit Dr. Harper. Unfortunately, she was not available. However, my sincere desire was to seek her redemption and approval, to thank her for motivating me to do better, and to let her know that she has been a significant influence on my life and career.

The entire staff — including Reggie Smith, Beverly Ford and David Frye — are true heroes. They have contributed immensely to the professional development and personal awareness of generations. God bless them all.

The Rev. Lonnie T. Stinson, of Indian Trail, N.C., is a retired U.S. Army command sergeant major and is currently assistant pastor of Mount Moriah Missionary Baptist Church in Matthews, N.C. After 30 years in uniform, he spent 10 years in federal service, culminating as the adjutant general of the Basic Combat Training Center of Excellence in Fort Jackson, S.C. While at UNCC from 1972-74, he and was a charter member of the Omega Psi Phi chapter. He earned a B.A. in business administration from Columbia College in 1988.

POSITIVE AND REAFFIRMING

By Phyllis A. Wingate

T he UNCC Black Studies program was my first exposure to many of the accomplishments of famous African-Americans. I grew up in a rural North Carolina county and attended segregated schools until I was in the 9th grade. African-American history was not being taught in my schools.

Even though my father went to Hood Theological Seminary (associated with Livingstone College at that time) and was a Baptist minister, we didn't talk much in our home about Black history and successful Black people.

Being part of the conversations, focus groups and the atmosphere created by the UNCC Black Studies program was so positive and reaffirming. I still remember the feeling of pride I had as a young Black woman as a result of these awakening experiences.

My first research paper in a psychology class was about the age at which children become aware of race. I never would have thought of this topic or felt empowered to ask this question had it not been for my exposure to the Black Studies program.

It was a confidence booster that contributed to my career success.

Phyllis A. Wingate, of Kannapolis, N.C., is a retired health-care executive who spent more than 40 years in senior leadership positions, recently as senior vice president of Atrium Health and president of Atrium Health Cabarrus in Concord, N.C. She served on the boards of the American Hospital Association and The Joint Commission on the Accreditation of Healthcare Organizations, as well as chaired the North Carolina Healthcare Association. She earned a B.S. in physical therapy from UNC-Chapel Hill in 1976 and a master's of health administration from Virginia Commonwealth University in 1981.

RESPONSIBILITY TO OTHERS

By Ezekiel Ben-Israel

B ertha Maxwell had to be just the kind of woman she was to deal with me, because I did not want to be in anybody's college.

I had planned to pack my car and head for the Deep South. I was going to spend the next year driving around the country, then go to an historically Black college or enlist in the Air Force.

I graduated from James Benson Dudley High School in Greensboro, N.C., on May 31, 1972. When it was my turn to shake the principal's hand and receive my diploma cover, my Dad stood up and gave me a letter from the University of North Carolina at Charlotte, informing me that I had been accepted and enrolled in summer school, beginning June 3.

My parents found out that I had not responded to several scholarship overtures, so they colluded and conspired with my favorite cousin, Trina Stowe, and I became a 49er.

Not long after I pulled onto campus, I scored a quarter-pound of Acapulco Gold. So, after class I knocked out my homework then partied on my floor and met new people.

I had my first contact with Dr. Maxwell in mid-September when I was summoned to her office. It struck me that she was like every one of the elder females in my life: nurturing, calming, authoritarian, efficient and productivity-driven.

Seems students were complaining that I was monopolizing classroom time and not allowing them to talk. In the segregated school system that I came out of, I was taught to fight for excellence, but the instructor controlled the class. I was not used to passive classmates. She listened to all my defenses until she had had enough, then she asked me what responsibility I had to my classmates.

I had no clue, and told her so. She taught me about community responsibility, how the strong are responsible for the weak and guarding the integrity of the whole. She taught me how to look beyond the surface of things to seek true motive, with the goal being to elevate the whole.

I trusted what she said and modified my behavior accordingly. She knew from our talks that I did not intend to stay there long, so she was always teaching me something.

The Black Studies Block taught me to assess my enemies' strengths and weaknesses, to effectively utilize my resources, to accurately calculate how actions will affect collateral communities, to strike in force, monitor and adjust, and to negotiate from strength.

I have served on several police abuse committees and found them rife with racism because they have to interface with the vilest of institutionalized racism: the criminal justice system. They always find a way for the cops to escape criminal charges, and the cash settlements would be purposely low to communicate that the United States of America does not value the life of a Black man.

I value every life, and I am fighting for every life.

Sometimes, that "giant leap for mankind" is one block at a time. Ujima.

◊ ◊ ◊

Ezekiel Ben-Israel (formerly Robert Benson Duren II), of Greensboro, N.C, is a community activist and an evangelist with the African Methodist Episcopal Zion Church. Since 1991, he has produced a twice-weekly cable TV program, "When Only the Truth Will Do." After attending UNCC from 1972-74 and pledging Omega Psi Phi, he earned a B.S. in industrial technology in manufacturing from North Carolina A&T State University in 1985 and an M.A. in counseling psychology from Oral Roberts University in 1988.

THROUGH TRIUMPHS AND STUMBLES

By Vanessa Gallman

A slave woman being raped by her master. That was the subject of an original poem I read during a Black Studies program luncheon. Halfway through, I noticed the invited university official sitting next to the podium was turning several shades of red while refusing to look at me.

By the time I read the last lines vowing murderous revenge, I was sure I had destroyed any goodwill Black Studies had on campus. I hastily added that the program had not only taught such tragic history but also how to focus positively on the future. It was far from a save.

I dared a look at Bertha Maxwell, program director. She sported that half smile that meant she was busy calculating her next moves.

I knew she would find a way to soothe the official I had ruffled or take full advantage of his discomfit.

Looking back on that embarrassment, I am amazed at all the opportunities the program gave me to showcase both talent and stumbles. And all because I was too lazy to fight the crowds lined up at rows of tables during freshman registration.

A new program, the Black Studies Block, offered one-stop scheduling for a semester of core courses. After the birth of a daughter prevented me from attending UNC-Chapel Hill right after high school, I just wanted to get enough credits to transfer there in two years.

But there is no way I would have prospered at such a large university without the education and nurturing I received from UNCC Black Studies teachers.

English professor Mary Harper introduced me to the Harlem Renaissance and allowed me to talk with prominent writers and activists who visited the campus.

Professor Beverly Ford took me to the Charlotte Observer newsroom to introduce me to an editor who would hire me for my first reporting job and, years later, my first editing job.

Professors Ann Carver and David Frye were the first white teachers I had ever met who were committed to Black advancement. And Bertha was a force of persistence and ingenuity.

Self-confidence and high expectations were the program's best gifts, especially during the second semester when we began to take half of our classes with other university students. Black Studies teachers stressed that we should sit in the front of lecture halls. For one white teacher, the sight of us staring in her face apparently was too intimidating. She actually cried at a meeting when sharing her unease.

I don't think we did anything different than other restless students taking a required class in the late afternoon. To get to the bottom of the matter, Bertha asked us to do to her what we might have been doing to the teacher. "We may be half-fools, but we're not whole fools," she recalls as my response.

I don't remember that so clearly, but there is no doubt I could be foolhardy with quips. Like the time the teachers honored me with the Harriet Tubman Award. "I deserve it," I said in an effort to appear nonchalant.

I still have that award. And I have tried to live up to it. Not just because of Tubman's legacy but because the teachers who gave it to me did so much to light my way through the wilderness of my youth.

◊ ◊ ◊

Vanessa Gallman, of Lexington, Ky., retired in 2019 as editorial page editor of the Lexington Herald-Leader. She pledged Delta Sigma Theta in 1974 at UNCC and earned a B.A. in journalism from UNC-Chapel Hill in 1976. She worked as a government editor for The Washington Post, a national correspondent for a newspaper chain and an assistant professor at Florida A&M University and the University of Maryland at College Park. Former president of the national organization for opinion writers, she chaired a Pulitzer Prize jury for editorial writing.

NURTURED, BUT CHALLENGED

By Boris Finch

My entrance into college was marked by anxieties beyond the norm. Within weeks of my high school graduation, I was struck with tuberculosis and spent four months and five days at a sanitorium for recovery.

As a result of my convalescence, I entered UNCC in spring 1973, a semester late. Upon registration for classes, l learned of what was referred to as the Black Studies Block.

The Block brought freshman students together under courses centered on liberal arts and African-American studies. We were a close-knit group within the program, and that served to make my matriculation an easier process.

Among the students in or out of the program, the most consistent topic of conversation related to faculty was program director Bertha Maxwell. Though her travels at that time prevented her from attending a day-to-day campus schedule, I quickly realized my peers had come to appreciate and rely on her leadership beyond the curriculum.

Once I met her, I, too, appreciated her commitment to the development of each of us as individuals. I regarded Bertha as the principal proponent of an essential program that nurtured and challenged students to optimal performance through greater understanding of African culture.

That mission has resonated in my life to this day. Many of the authors and subjects that were introduced to me in the program in 1973 have proven relevant and significant in present-day observations of Africans throughout the diaspora.

We all owe a debt of gratitude to her excellent work in advancing the study of the Black experience in our world.

◊ ◊ ◊

Boris Finch of Charlotte is owner of Finch Enterprises, which has offered packaged food entrees, bottled water and other consumables to commercial and residential customers since 1990. At UNCC, he pledged Omega Psi Phi. He chose to become an independent contractor with sales and marketing corporations before starting his own company.

NO LONGER A VICTIM

By Cynthia Mullen Stewart

I grew up in Jackson, Miss., in a neighborhood near the home of civil rights leader Medgar Evers and attended a church where Freedom Riders slept overnight in our Sunday School room.

As a freshman, I attended Michigan State University, which had 40,000 students on campus at that time. Having grown up in the Deep South, the climate at Michigan State — meteorologically, culturally, socially, politically and educationally — was not a good fit for me, and I struggled.

I spent most of my freshman year applying for acceptance and financial aid at smaller Southern universities. I transferred to UNCC my sophomore year. During my first semester there, I was a student in the Black Studies program.

The course content led to an epiphany for me, reinforcing pride in my race and the boundless resourcefulness of Black people. It gave Black students a sense of community. And where I had floundered in the massive impersonality and coldness of MSU, I was provided a campus family at UNCC with Black Studies director Bertha Maxwell firmly established as our matriarch and peers with whom I developed lifelong connections.

Between Bertha and Dr. Dee Sanders in the College of Nursing, I was supported, nurtured and encouraged to work hard, do my best and to succeed. There were only six African-American students in my nursing class of nearly 100. We relied on one another, our friends in other majors and Bertha heavily. Her office was always open to us as a respite and a gathering place.

At times we had grievances or situations that we needed to navigate on campus. Bertha never babied us but was always a ready sounding board to listen and guide us in developing plans to address problems and effect our own resolutions. She taught us we were capable of dreaming big and solving big problems.

The course changed how I viewed myself. I no longer thought of myself only as a "victim" of racism. Through the course and my faith in God, I learned to see myself as a powerful proponent of my own needs and achievement — even in a racist setting.

Confident enough during my senior year to have a big graduate school dream, I applied for and was awarded a U.S. Public Health Service traineeship to attend Duke University. I was the first African-American student to graduate from Duke's School of Nursing master of science program.

Bertha has been a blessing, a supporter and encourager in my life. I am grateful to know her.

◊ ◊ ◊

Cynthia Mullen Stewart, of Missouri City, Texas, retired in 2012 after 35 years with the University of Texas MD Anderson Cancer Center in Houston, serving most recently as a clinical administrative. She is the 1991 recipient of the Brown Foundation Award for Excellence in Oncology Nursing. After receiving a B.S. in nursing from UNCC in

1975, she earned an M.A. in nursing from Duke University in 1976. While at UNCC, she was a charter member of the Iota Rho chapter of Delta Sigma Theta Sorority.

CONFIDENCE TO COMPETE

By Ed Flowers

My experience in the UNCC Black Studies program was profound and long-lasting from a life and career perspective. Arriving on campus in 1973 was not only a big transition from high school, I was trying the make the up-and-coming Division I basketball team as a walk-on.

It was somewhat overwhelming trying to navigate through getting the right classes and learning how to manage social life on campus.

Bertha Maxwell and the Black Studies team presented the opportunity to transition into college with people who looked like me. I found the program very enlightening in terms of education and learning.

However, the main thing was that it allowed me to have the confidence to compete and graduate in an environment that was not always fair and friendly toward African-Americans.

My career has been impacted by that experience. While navigating through corporate executive roles as the only African-American in many Fortune 500 companies, I still remember my days at UNCC and the confidence I gained in the Black Studies program.

As a chief human resources officer in several major companies, I credit my success to my experiences in the Black Studies program as a foundation to my accomplishments.

Well done, Bertha.

Ed Flowers of Atlanta is managing partner of consumer, human resources and diversity practices in the Atlanta office of DHR, an executive search firm. He has held top executive positions in international companies such as Corelle Brands and Monsanto. He earned a B.A. in history with a minor in business administration from UNCC in 1977. He also has completed an executive management program at Wharton School of Business and an executive human resources program at the University of Michigan. He is a member of Kappa Alpha Psi Fraternity.

TRUE BONDING EXPERIENCE

By Theresa Graves

It was fall 1973 when I arrived on the campus of UNCC. My dad and his friend dropped me off at the curb between the newly constructed Holshouser and Sanford dorms, where I was prepared to spend the next four years of my life.

I had never spent the night away from my parents for more than a week. At the curb, I was met by a welcoming committee of Black upperclassmen. My first surprise! You see, I had never visited the campus, so I didn't know what to expect. That really made me feel welcome, and my anxiety was reduced immediately.

Skip to the start of my classes. UNCC had the largest enroll-ment of Black students that year. Thankfully, Bertha Maxwell and Herman Thomas arranged for all Black freshmen to opt into required courses that were geared more toward Afrocentric classes, or "Block" classes as we called them.

Bertha, Herman and Mary Harper worked together to spear-head the African-American and African Studies Department. The classes were scheduled and taught by people who looked like us.

With the majority of Black freshmen taking classes together, it really helped bond us and kept us strong as we navigated our way around a predominantly white campus.

An added benefit for me is that I learned how significant Black Americans' roles were in U.S. history. The pride that I felt and the resulting lessons learned have stuck with me all these years.

I know now that had it not been for my experience, I would have been so very unprepared to take on the world as I did. I grew from a shy sheltered girl to a brave, bold woman over the four years under the program's wing, and I am so very grateful.

Theresa Graves, of High Point, N.C., retired after 30 years as a project manager in the financial industry, including as first building manager for Southern Bell in Chapel Hill. She also worked in the Hollywood film industry as a financial analyst. She earned a B.A, in business administration from UNCC in 1977 and project management professional credentials in 2006. She was a charter member of UNCC's Kappa Kappa chapter of Alpha Kappa Alpha.

TRADITION OF EXCELLENCE

By Kevin T. King

My experiences at UNC Charlotte were some of my most gratifying. I remember as an 18-year-old freshman finally getting away from home and going to a place where I didn't know anyone, except for meeting my basketball teammates.

I was introduced to the Black Studies program by some teammates who were involved in the program, and I registered for the classes offered to freshmen, called "The Block," and met director Bertha Maxwell Roddey and other professors such as Herman Thomas, Mary Harper and Beverly Ford.

Dr. Maxwell stood out due to her overwhelming presence, as she instructed several of the classes. She also gracefully showed and taught me about Black history; how Black people had a rich tradition; and how we impacted American society by creating inventions and businesses, as well as producing great actors, writ-ers; the list goes on and on.

After graduation, I always came back to see Dr. Maxwell to inform her that she was a positive influence in my life and career. The lessons she taught me about doing the right thing and having integrity remain present today.

I can honestly say I'm thankful for the Black Studies program and glad I had the experience of being part of it.

Kevin T. King, of Mt. Gilead, N.C., has worked with the North Carolina Department of Public Safety since 1982 and currently is warden of the Southern Correctional Institution in Troy. He is also a retired master sergeant in the U.S. Army Reserve. He earned a B.A. in human services from UNCC in 1979 and an M.A. in public admin-istration from Webster University at Fort Bragg in 2004. From 1975-79, he was a member of the UNCC men's basketball team, which played in the finals of the National Invitation Tournament in 1976 and was in the 1977 NCAA Final Four. He is a member of Kappa Alpha Psi Fraternity.

MOVING VISIT TO AFRICA

By Sheryl Westmoreland

Of the many wonderful experiences that I had as a UNCC student, my participation in the New York-based African-American Institute's six-week Educators to Africa Student Study Abroad Program would be considered extraordinary.

The tour included travel to three West African countries: Ghana, Togo and Benin; Nigeria was an optional addition of the package.

Drs. Bertha Maxwell, Herman Thomas, Mary Harper and Ann Carver of the Black Studies department met frequently with me and classmates L. Diane Bennett and Robert "Bobby" Flowers to present us with an international summer travel opportunity.

Through their tireless efforts, as well as scholarship assistance from church members and local community leaders, our travel and miscellaneous expenses were covered. I will be forever grateful for the fish fries, the donations and hard work my parents and relatives contributed to make my first abroad experience come true.

During the early morning of July 7, 1976, Diane, Bobby and I said farewells to crowds of friends and family and prepared to board a jet to New York. Suddenly, I realized that within two days I would walk on African soil. Nervous and extremely scared, I said aloud, "I can't do this." A voice from somewhere in the crowd responded, "Girl, you better get on that plane!"

Thanks to my travel companions, I was able to smile my way through the anxiety and board the plane.

Upon our arrival in New York, we were introduced to about 20 academicians from various areas of the continental United States. Many were graduate students of African-American history and literature who were researching the final portions of their dissertations; others were department chairs and interested travelers. African-Americans and Africans comprised the majority of our group. Diane, Bobby and I were among the youngest.

After a two-hour layover in Monrovia, we arrived in Accra and were transported to our lodging at the University of Cape Coast. Our itinerary included daily classroom instruction by various university professors, as well as meal, travel and personal time.

An experience that remains strongly in my memory was our tour of Elmina Castle. The structure was huge, dark and haunting while overlooking the massive Atlantic Ocean. It had been a site for kidnapped Africans who were kept there and sold to slave hunters arriving by ships. This was an extremely intense and emotionally draining experience for the African-Americans on the tour. We became quiet, distant; conversation was non-existent as our guide led us through the many slave-holding cells.

Non-Black members of our group (in their discomfort to our reactions), began making light-hearted conversation among themselves. They were reprimanded immediately by African-American members of our group for their lack of sensitivity and respect for the castle's tragic history. Many of the companionships and newly established friendships among us were severely strained thereafter, only to be reconciled within the last few weeks of the trip.

Finally, this was the first time I celebrated my birthday twice within a 27-hour period. As a result of our timely departure from Africa during the week of Aug. 18, I was thrilled to celebrate my birthday once on African soil and, hours later, in the United States.

It was an awesome ending to a most unbelievable summer experience. I was — and remain — grateful to all who made it happen.

◊ ◊ ◊

Sheryl LeVerne Westmoreland (Smith) of Charlotte is a retired college instructor. She taught in the First Year Writing Program at Winston-Salem State University for 16 years; English, rhetoric and world literature at Belmont Abbey College for 14 years; and African-American and African Studies at UNCC for three years. After receiving her B.A. at UNCC in 1977, she earned an M.A. from the University of Iowa in 1980. She also studied at North Carolina A&T State University and Central Piedmont Community College. She is a member of UNCC's Iota Rho Chapter of Delta Sigma Theta Sorority.

UNYIELDING SUPPORT

By Terry L. Smith

I am fortunate to have been recruited into the original Black Studies program class of UNCC in August 1972. It was an awesome experience that helped me and other students matriculate into the UNC system that wasn't sure how to support us, or whether it really wanted us there.

Bertha chose a team of instructors who gave me the unyielding support I needed as I sought to define "Who am I?" My experiences formed a foundation of self-confidence that thoroughly prepared me for the real world and the ongoing and not-so-subtle racism that remains almost 50 years later.

I learned to love me as I am, and am forever grateful for beginning my transition to adulthood with my fellow "first mates." I love you for this!

◊ ◊ ◊

Terry L. Smith, of Burke, Va., has spent a 40-year career in the management of commercial liability claims, currently working for Washington Metropolitan Area Transit Authority in the District of Columbia. He earned a B.A. in business administration from UNCC in 1976.

POSITIVE CHANGE

By Brenda Edwards Jones

M y experience as a student of "The Block," as it was called, was positive. It proved to be a nurturing environment that went beyond the classroom. It has had lasting effects on my life.

I was always in awe of the powerful Black women such as Dr. Bertha Maxwell Roddey and Dr. Beverly Ford. They were so accomplished and classy. All the professors were kind and approachable.

The entire experience greatly helped me while being in a predominantly white institution. It instilled the confidence that helped me with the career paths I chose and life's challenges. I feel I made the right choice.

Dr. Roddey is such a powerful force and motivator who made you want to be a better you and to effect positive change in the world.

◊ ◊ ◊

Brenda Edwards Jones, of Raleigh, N.C., retired from Wake County Human Services and is a Mary Kay consultant. She earned a B.A. in sociology and education from UNCC in 1978. A U.S. Air Force veteran active with Disabled American Veterans, she is founder of an investment club, a volunteer for Dress for Success and a member of Delta Sigma Theta Sorority.

ON SOLID FOUNDATION

By Avis Houston Wilson

In 1973, I entered UNCC as the second person in my family to attend college. But still, I was not equipped to navigate this educational experience. I was a native Charlottean, a commuter student and the single parent of a 4-month-old.

As such, my experience was very different from that of most of the freshman in my class. Within the Black Studies program, I found Bertha, Mary, Herman, Roberta and classmates who truly helped this scared freshman to flourish and succeed.

The program offered the foundation of a solid education, plus safe boundaries; and it opened my eyes/insight into history and experiences that I had not been exposed to.

While at UNCC I participated in the Black Student Union, was director of fine arts and lectures for the Union Program Board, and became a charter member of the Kappa Kappa Chapter for Alpha Kappa Alpha Sorority.

◊ ◊ ◊

Avis Houston Wilson, of Concord, N.C., retired after 38 years in the banking industry, recently as a senior vice president and technology executive for Bank of America. She currently works as a tax consultant and a real estate investor. For more than 25 years, she has served as trustee of Marvin A.M.E. Zion Church in Waxhaw, N.C. She graduated from UNCC in 1977 with a B.A. in business administration and received additional technology certificates through Villanova University.

INSPIRATION MIXED WITH FUN

By Robert Rowell

During my four-year tenure at UNCC (1977-81), the Black Studies Department played a major role in my growth and development as a student. It also carried over into my professional life in the financial services industry.

I took several courses in the department through The Block, which allowed me to meet fellow Black students, as we were all in this together to graduate from a predominantly white institution. This gave me the opportunity to take my freshman literature class under Dr. Mary Harper, who exposed me to "Invisible Man" by Ralph Ellison and "The Autobiography of Malcolm X: As Told to Alex Haley."

Learning how to articulate my thoughts about these books and put them on paper had a major impact on my writing skills.

The department exposed us to many famous and influential African-Americans, including Dr. Benjamin Hooks, Dick Gregory, Ruby Dee and Ossie Davis, Nikki Giovanni, the Rev. Jesse Jackson, Minister Louis Farrakhan and the Rev. Ralph Abernathy. Seeing and hearing giants such as these inspired me to work even harder in school and in my corporate life.

Though we didn't have a lot of Black students during my time at UNCC, I didn't feel alone and isolated because of the Black Studies Department, and being a member of Alpha Phi Alpha Fraternity and the Children of the Sun gospel choir.

We had some memorable basement dorm parties for 50 cents, and big parties in the Lucas Room. We had the Jam-Up Festival concerts with Mother's Finest and the Average White Band, competitive Greek intramural basketball games and step shows we still talk about today.

I'd do it all over again with no regrets. 49er forever!

Robert Rowell of Charlotte retired in 2009 as vice president/investments for Wells Fargo Advisors. A 1981 UNCC graduate with a B.A. in business administration, he was awarded a UNCC Black Alumni Chapter Excellence in Leadership Award in 2018. He was named a Five Star Wealth Manager by Charlotte Magazine and was highlighted in the 2019 publication "Who's Who in Black Charlotte."

SOURCE OF BALANCE, AFFIRMATION

By Gerald Jeanette Little

U NCC was not my choice for college, but, in retrospect, it was the right space for me.

Being a native Charlottean and graduate of Black-only West Charlotte Senior High, my introduction to the world of diversity was about to begin. My time on campus was limited because of commuting and outside employment. The challenge of meeting new people, transitioning into this new world of independence and completing educational requirements for a career became a refreshing new goal.

The Black Studies program provided a platform of balance between learning a new culture while staying in touch with my own.

I remember two new friends — one an AKA, the other a Delta — inviting me to pledge their sororities. I was torn. So, in the spirit of compromise, I chose to remain neutral, declaring myself a "Non Phi Non."

The melodious a cappella sound of the newly formed gospel choir reminded me of my spiritual roots and younger days. That was inspiring. But I also can remember being on campus all day and not seeing any of "us." That was hard.

However, my most memorable days at UNCC — my "never-will-forget days" — were spent in Dr. Bertha Maxwell Roddey's class. At that time, the focus was on newly enacted laws regarding affirmative action. I learned the significance of affirmative action and how it affected Blacks in this country. It became clear to me why so many, including myself, had been afforded the opportunity to not only attend UNCC but to receive financial assistance as well.

In the years after my graduation, I observed many Caucasian colleagues and associates who had no credentials, lacked experience and were unprofessional yet were given the opportunity to progress in their careers. During these times, I reflected on Dr. Roddey's class.

I often now envision our flower garden of Black people, including my parents, who were hard workers, who deserved wearing the titles of supervisor, office manager, owner, etc. But racism denied them such opportunities.

I remember those discussions on affirmative action when I cross paths with brothers, sisters and other people of color who are excelling in every walk of life and making extraordinary contributions to society.

Affirmative action was about numbers. Today it's about having an equal voice at the table. Dr. Roddey reminded us that, in life, every positive has a negative. She advised that for future reference, we should listen for the term "reverse discrimination."

The first time I publicly heard that term — 20-plus years later — I remembered the class and immediately shouted, "Bertha Maxwell!"

The depth of her insight is matchless. Just as I remember how the UNCC Black Studies program impacted my life, I will forever appreciate her.

◊ ◊ ◊

Gerald Jeanette Little of Charlotte worked 22 years as an insurance claims representative and arbitration specialist based in Dallas, Texas. After graduating from UNCC with a B.A. in sociology in 1974, she worked as a counselor for Planned Parenthood Charlotte. Before retiring, she was a teacher assistant in Charlotte public schools.

SECTION III

LEARNING FROM BERTHA

BEACON FOR EXCELLENCE

By Arthur Griffin Jr.

"Frère Jacques, Frère Jacques, Dormez-vous? Dormez-vous?"

That French jingle was forever etched into my memory by my fourth-grade experience and teacher.

Bertha Maxwell, the young Johnson C. Smith University graduate, was clearly one of the best teachers at Charlotte's First Ward Elementary during the late 1950s. She was immensely popular and very well-dressed. She was caring and competent, with high expectations for her students in a very segregated school setting.

Bertha and I lived in the same community. She got to know my father and became aware of his illiteracy. She forged a personal relationship with all her students. She made us feel comfortable with her focus on excellence in the classroom. If we got out of line, she would pinch our ears.

She taught us French before a foreign language was part of the standard curriculum because she wanted us to have dreams.

Fast forward decades later, at the University of North Carolina at Charlotte, where I would find myself again a student of that same caring and competent teacher. This time, in the Afro-American and African Studies Department.

Long before Ancestry.com, Bertha wanted us to know, understand and appreciate our African-American heritage. She and her colleagues became the lighthouse, a beacon in the middle of a big white education ocean. She guided each us to reach our fullest potential and to become who we are today.

Often, her office was a place you would go to get your "get out of jail" card. It was a place to reset after a difficult test or school challenge. You could always count on Bertha's counsel, listening ear and shoulder to cry on.

Finally, I give credit to Bertha's guidance for my life's focus on equity and equality, and for many of my personal achievements. She persuaded me to work with her and her colleague Dr. Mary Harper in setting up the Afro-American Cultural Center at Little Rock Church in Charlotte.

That experience crystallized my commitment to racial justice. She opened the door for an internship and subsequent job at the Legal Aid Society.

From there, I never looked back. Thank you, Bertha.

Arthur Griffin Jr. of Charlotte is a retired senior vice president of McGraw-Hill Education in New York. He served on the Charlotte-Mecklenburg Board of Education, including as chair from 1997-2002. He also chaired Charlotte's Black Political Caucus. A Vietnam veteran and retired lieutenant colonel in the U.S. Army, he attended UNCC from 1972-74 and earned a B.S. in liberal studies from The University of the State of New York in 1992.

SELF-AFFIRMING MANTRA

By Winnie McNeely Bennett

Perhaps my strongest memory of Dr. Bertha Maxwell is of her telling the young Black men and women in her class to look in the mirror at ourselves daily.

"Really look," she would say. "And say to yourself, 'I am a beautiful, proud, smart Black woman/man.'"

I have repeated that mantra many, many times. I have said it when I was looked over for a promotion, when someone said something negative to me or about me, and when I've even been down on myself.

Dr. Maxwell encouraged us to seek for ourselves, to go on this journey to understand who we were, where we came from and where we were going.

When I entered UNC Charlotte, I was among the cohort of Black students integrating predominantly white schools in the

1960s; I had helped in 1966 to integrate Monroe High School in Monroe, N.C.

It was quite difficult being part of those first groups of students. There was hostility, coolness and prejudice. In fact, the mascot of my high school was the "Rebels." So, by the time I entered UNCC, I was a little battle-worn; my spirits were low and my expectations of attending another integrated institution were not great. But UNCC was recruiting Black students and had provided enough financial support.

Perhaps Dr. Maxwell knew this, intuitively, about all of the Black students who entered in the late 1960s and early 1970s. She knew we needed to figure out who we were to determine how to navigate a world not friendly to us.

So, she equipped us with knowledge and skills, and she reminded us of our history and how our experiences as Black Americans had shaped us. She told us to always be proud of who we were and who our ancestors were, as their struggle brought us to where we were at that time.

In all of the positions I have held since I left UNCC, I utilized the important principles and knowledge I gained from the Black Studies program and from the director of that program. In almost every major decision I had to make during my career and often in my personal life, I heard Dr. Maxwell's voice in my ear telling me, "You know who you are."

◊ ◊ ◊

Winnie McNeely Bennett, of Morven, N.C., is a retired supervisor with the Union County Department of Social Services. She also worked as an instructor of human services at South Piedmont Community College for 20 years. She earned a B.A. in sociology from UNCC in 1974 and a master of social work from Case Western Reserve University in 1978. She has served on community boards and organizations, including as a founding member of the Morven Chapter of Las Amigas Inc., a women's civic group.

PERPETUAL INFLUENCE

By Staccato Powell

T he most impactful academic influence in my journey of life
was the African-American and African Studies Department, as
it was known in the early 1980s, at the University of North Carolina
at Charlotte.

This experience was personified through the iconic personality
of Bertha Maxwell, the department chair. Due to Bertha's win-
some way, I was persuaded to double major in political science and
African-American and African Studies.

During the introduction course, Bertha related she was from
Seneca, S.C. She knew most people had not heard of the town.
However, Bertha declared it was imperative for an individual to
acknowledge and embrace the place where they are from in order
to get to where they are going.

From that moment forward, I proudly shared that I hailed from Hallsboro, N.C. When people respond by saying they have not heard of the place or do not know where it is, I retort by emphasizing they are geographically challenged.

One does not have to be astute to know New York City, but only the brightest will know the insignificant spots on the globe. Bertha's teaching by percept and example instilled within many of us a healthy sense of self.

Those of us who took advantage of the safe haven provided through the department discovered academic success more readily. Bertha ensured we enrolled in core courses taught by professors whom she personally vetted to support students of African descent.

Venerable and iconic personalities such as professors Mary Harper and Ann Carver taught English. Herman Thomas was my academic adviser and guided me through UNCC and encouraged me to attend Duke University Divinity School for my master of divinity.

Just being able to go into the Rowe Building and bound up the stairs to the second floor, where the department's offices were located, was like coming out of the rain to be refreshed.

Even until this day I cherish memories of those days from 1978 to 1980 on the campus of UNCC and continue the relationships established.

Two of my trusted friends and colleagues in ministry are Herman Thomas and Gregory Davis, both of whom are mentors I met through Bertha and the department. Roberta P. Duff, the administrative assistant, was and is a great source of encouragement along the way.

Words are poor tools to adequately express the positive and perpetual impact Dr. Bertha Maxwell Roddey has had on my life.

At the invitation of Herman Thomas, I was invited to preach at a worship service at a Charlotte church in December 2019. To my delight, Bertha graced us with her presence. May God continue to grant her enormous favor for the many lives she impacted.

Staccato Powell, of Sacramento, Calif., has served 44 years in ministry and is presently presiding bishop of Western Episcopal District of the African Methodist Episcopal Zion Church. He earned a B.A. from UNCC in 1980, a masters of divinity from Duke University and a juris doctor from North Carolina Central University. He has served as deputy general secretary of the National Council of Churches, as president and CEO of OIC of America, on the World Council of Churches Central Committee, as president of the AMEZ Board of Bishops and as grand chaplain of Omega Psi Phi Fraternity.

AN ORGANIZING PRINCIPLE

By Gaile Dry-Burton

I grew up in Nyack, N.Y., a small village 30 miles outside of New York City. I knew little to nothing about my African culture and heritage. Dr. Bertha Maxwell Roddey's encouragement helped me earn a bachelor's of arts degree in African-American and African Studies and psychology.

The double major required presenting a thesis to a committee comprised of a faculty member from each discipline, as well as someone from the community. Well, I was procrastinating, struggling with finding the best topic, forming the committee, etcetera. One day, Dr. Roddey asked me if I had started my thesis.

It was still in my head, I responded.

She gave me a firm look and stated: "Girl, if it ain't in writing, it ain't!"

Those words etched into my mind. It occurred to me that every time I thought about my thesis project it would change, always bringing me back to square one of uncertainty. I began the writing process and, of course, the thesis took form. I began writing lists and, sure enough, I completed every item.

It was like the words were pictures of what would be.

I have written and repeated "if it ain't in writing …" at every training class I presented for 20 years working for AT&T.

Dr. Roddey also instilled in me a deep pride, reminding me that my culture is rich, and my heritage extends from African kings and queens and did not begin as slaves forced to work on plantations in America.

Her wisdom, her shoulders are what I stand on and what make me the person I am today. I will continue to carry her legacy forward.

Dr. Gaile Dry-Burton of Charlotte worked 32 years with AT&T, primarily in human resources, training and development. She recently retired from a 13-year second career as a schoolteacher. After receiving her B.A. from UNCC in 1983, she earned an M.A. in human resources training and development at Seton Hall University in 2002, a M.A. in teaching from UNCC in 2009 and a doctorate of education leadership from University of Phoenix in 2018. She is a member of Delta Sigma Theta Sorority, Inc.

PREPARED FOR OPPORTUNITIES

By B. Stanley Graham

In 1961, I began my fifth-grade year at First Ward Elementary School in Charlotte. Customarily, students waited on the hard-top of the playground for teachers to call their rolls. The younger students were called first and followed teachers to their respective classrooms. It seemed like it took forever to get to my grade.

One of my peers brought a ball to school, and we thought we would play some before they called for us. Bad idea. I did not tear my clothes or get dirty, but I did get sweaty. A staff member repri-manded us, reminding us of our purpose for attending school. As I looked over potential teachers, all were "pretty cool," but one stood out. I really wanted to be in her class.

Watch what you wish for, right?

I heard my name called. I was now in Mrs. Bertha Maxwell's class, so I took my place in line. Her classroom was immaculate, inviting. Her demeanor, charm and passion for teaching kept students very attentive. We kept our focus on doing our best. She cultivated an environment for learning, self-esteem and character-building.

I got a chance to take band that year. I had long discovered my love for music and now, looking back, I can say I built the foundation of who I am from the teachings, inspiration and encouragement of Mrs. Maxwell.

I will never forget winning a contest dancing The Twist. After returning to class, Mrs. Maxwell surprised me by taking me to other teachers to show my "winning moves." I closed my eyes and "worked it out" as they enjoyed my demonstration.

The year ended on a great note, then I learned Mrs. Maxwell had signed me up for a summer school for gifted and talented students in math, science and the arts. Bummer! One consolation: There was music and physical education. I grudgingly attended.

I was too young to realize the value, exposure and great opportunity the camp was giving me. However, after the words Mrs. Maxwell shared with my parents and me, I was determined to do better from that point on.

Fast forward to the 1970s. I am a student at the University of North Carolina at Charlotte majoring in music and minoring in sociology. We reunite, with her loving smile and a big hug like the ones I remember from elementary school.

As a senior preparing to graduate, I found myself still learning valuable lessons from her. She literally helped me get myself organized by establishing purpose, the value of using a calendar, time management, short- and long-term goal setting, utilization of resources and working with people from diverse backgrounds.

She has constantly demonstrated love, compassion and a genuine interest in student well-being and success. Two lessons from her: You must prepare for opportunities, and you must show people what you can do. She has been a constant resource for counsel, inspiration, wisdom and encouragement.

I am thankful to God for Dr. Bertha Maxwell Roddey for how she has richly blessed my life and many others'. Much love and peace.

◊ ◊ ◊

B. Stanley Graham of Charlotte is a professional musician who also worked 30 years in public health and human services, including directing a family planning program for males and neighborhood-based social services. He has toured with stage plays, recorded and performed for singers Joe Simon, Nappy Brown, Ashford & Simpson, and the Rivieras. He composed the music for the West Charlotte High School documentary, "The Mighty Lions," and performed on-screen in the film, "The Color Purple." Past board member for Queen City Brass and the Charlotte Pops Orchestra, he received in 2002 an award for lifetime musical excellence from Charlotte's Afro-American Cultural Center. He also served in leadership roles in the Presbyterian Church (USA) from 1996-2000.

MATERNAL EMBRACE

By Phaedra Berry Holley

In August 1970, a young lady from Kinston, N.C., was left on the campus by her parents to begin a new phase of her life. Being approximately 300 miles from home and knowing absolutely no one in Charlotte, I immediately had to begin to embrace my new situation.

After being acclimated to dorm life, forming new lifelong friendships, I began my class experience. The class that had the most impact on my life was Black Experience under the tutelage of Dr. Bertha Maxwell Roddey, leader of the Black Studies program.

She embraced us with love, sternness and persuasion. She became the most-needed "Mom" away from home. Not only did she teach us how to survive as Black students on a predominantly white campus, she taught us how to survive in the world that we know today.

We spent countless hours in her office, above and beyond the required class time. She served as our counselor, our cheerleader, our encourager, our sounding board and, if necessary, our disciplinarian.

She taught us how to stand up for ourselves and fight for justice, taking on projects with activists T.J. Reddy and Ben Chavis and for the freedom of the wrongly imprisoned Wilmington Ten.

In addition to being a major influence in my overall adult development, she had the most impact when she helped 13 phenomenal women charter the Iota Rho Chapter of Delta Sigma Theta Sorority.

Dec. 2, 1972, will be engraved forever in my heart and soul as it marks the accomplishment of a lifelong dream realized under her leadership. She started my life in Delta and has continued to be a strong advocate and influence in my Delta walk for almost 48 years.

I really cannot imagine what my life would be like today had I not been blessed with her guidance and the family I acquired from matriculating at UNCC.

Phaedra Berry Holley, of Kinston, N.C., retired after 36 years of teaching math in middle school and community college, is an adjunct college instructor. She earned a B.A. in mathematics from UNCC in 1973 and a master's of art in education specializing in mathematics from East Carolina University. She has served in many local and regional capacities in Delta Sigma Theta Sorority.

PAYING IT FORWARD

By Sanford Jerome Wingate

"The quality, not the longevity, of one's life is what's important." — Martin Luther King Jr.

Bertha Maxwell's impact on the lives of so many is unmeasurable. Important to me was learning through the Black Studies program the many contributions of Afro-Americans throughout history.

It changed my life to know that with dedication, hard work and perseverance I could build a future for me and a family.

I have had opportunity to recruit, hire, mentor and promote others like me. My goal was to "pay it forward" while working within the corporate structure to ensure others had opportunities to succeed.

Through being part of the UNCC program, I learned the idea that I can succeed as a Black man in business, and be a present father and husband.

Thanks for Bertha's leadership.

◊ ◊ ◊

Sanford Jerome Wingate of Charlotte retired in 2013 after a 35-year career with AT&T, most recently as North Carolina manager for advertising sales. He received a bachelor's degree from UNCC in 1974 and was instrumental in bringing Epsilon Zeta Chapter of Omega Psi Fraternity to the campus, serving as its first president.

EMPOWERED FOR CHANGE

By Elaine Nichols

D r. Bertha Maxwell Roddey was a leader who connected with students as a teacher, friend, confidant and mentor. One of her greatest impacts was that she empowered students to think for themselves, to demonstrate excellence and to make positive changes to society. For the Black students, she always affirmed our value as human beings who were part of a legacy of people who made significant contributions to America and the world.

Elaine Nichols of Charlotte is supervisory curator of culture at the Smithsonian National Museum of African American History and Culture. She was a curator at the South Carolina State Museum and a city planner for Cleveland, Ohio. After earning a B.A. in political science at UNCC, she received a master's of science in social

administration at Case Western Reserve University and an M.A. in public service archaeology at the University of South Carolina.

LEADER WORTH FOLLOWING

By Warren Peacock

I attended UNCC during a time when many of us represented the first generation in our families to enroll in college. There were few, if any, people we could seek out to obtain advise and helpful hints as to what to expect.

Within a few days of officially stepping foot on campus, we met a dynamo of a person in the name of Bertha Maxwell, who immediately assumed the role and responsibility. Her persona was welcoming and impactful as she exhibited a genuine and focused desire for each of us to reach our fullest potential.

She ultimately would develop into a mentor, cheerleader, nurturer, confidant and, for many, an academic advisor.

There were only approximately 1,000 Black students on campus during that time. The African-American and African Studies Department that Bertha and her staff spearheaded provided the opportunity to transition into the college experience academically and socially.

We followed the AAA curriculum through at least our sophomore year, with many obtaining their bachelor's through the program. Interacting with one another daily through classes, studying and socializing, and formalizing consistent relationships with AAA professors provided the collective support that would not have existed otherwise.

The totality of the experience is why we reflect so fondly on the time we learned and grew together during those critical formative years. It is also why we have maintained such close bonds that have now stretched 40-plus years.

Bertha's influence on the lives of the people she's touched worldwide is immeasurable. We are all truly blessed having come her way and to be noted as "Bertha Disciples."

Warren Peacock, of Durham, N.C., is executive vice president of branch operations for the State Employees' Credit Union (SECU), overseeing 270 branches and 5,700 employees. He earned his B.A. in business administration from UNCC in 1982 and was the first Black senior vice president and executive vice president at SECU, the world's second-largest credit union.

PASSION FOR HELPING

By Barbara A. Washington

I was at UNCC from 1971-75 and was privileged and honored to be a student, mentee and admirer of Dr. Bertha Maxwell Roddey.

It still amazes me that a person with so many notable accomplishments spent — and is still spending — so much of her life giving to, uplifting, teaching and encouraging generations.

I think one of her most notable characteristics is humility. She puts herself out there as "Just Bertha" but always has made major contributions to local and national causes.

I'm a better person because of Dr. Roddey and her passion for helping, her living to be a blessing, and because of the example she lived before me as a stellar role model.

The career and life successes I've experienced were due in part to the things imparted to me by Dr. Roddey: integrity, a God-centered existence, godly character, passion, courage, focus, compassion, selflessness, endurance, self-worth and purpose.

Bertha, I'm sincerely grateful for you and your impartations that are still affecting my life and the lives of many others.

◊ ◊ ◊

Barbara A. Washington of Charlotte retired after a 35-year career, focused on banking, with the U.S. Department of the Treasury. She earned a B.A. in business administration from UNCC in 1975 and ran her own religious book publishing company during the 1990s.

SAGE WITH A POWERFUL LEGACY

By Ronald S. Swann

As a former student and lecturer in the College of Humanities in the Black Studies Department, I consider it an honor and a privilege to contribute to the legacy of Bertha, which is what she wanted students to call her. I am more than proud to have been considered one of "Bertha's Young Men," in addition to Robert Bernard Reeves, Ben Chavis, T.J. Reddy and the Rev. Gregory Davis.

I graduated from Ben L. Smith High School in Greensboro, N.C., in 1966 and from Gaston College in Dallas, N.C., in 1969 with an associate of arts degree. I decided to transfer to UNCC after attending a UNCC basketball game at UNC Greensboro and realizing that the team's freshman star, Norris Dae, was African-American. It was an omen for me.

There had been a protest on the campus in the form of the "Ten Demands," led by Chavis and others on Feb. 26, 1969. One demand was for a Black Studies program controlled by Black students and staffed by Black faculty. I enrolled in fall 1969 and began my exposure to Bertha, a sage who assisted students in discovering important truths about the world and themselves.

Once enrolled in the Black Perspective course, students had an option to attend an encounter retreat on campus with staff, faculty and students to understand their roles in dealing with systemic racism in education, defusing potential problems and learning there is strength in numbers.

During the encounter, the tenets of the Black Studies program were explored: Who am I? Where did I come from? Why am I here? Where do I go from here? The grand finale of the retreat was a social get-together at The Excelsior Club.

In spring 1970, I was elected president of the Black Student Union and became a member of Kappa Alpha Psi Fraternity along with nine brothers. Bertha, a member of Delta Sigma Theta Sorority, encouraged us, despite the outcry of some students who saw fraternities as irrelevant.

While taking Black Studies classes, students had to do an internship, which I did at Hidden Valley Elementary. My first job after graduation, as a counselor at Johnson C. Smith University, seemed a logical step for me.

In 1975, when I returned to UNCC to work as a lecturer in Black Studies, I honed new skills under Bertha's leadership. I was a liaison to various administrative committees on campus. I attended meetings with the dean of Creative Arts where there were discussions about innovations in instruction, and adjusting curriculum and learning process in accordance with student needs.

Bertha often talked of growing up in Seneca, S.C., being raised by a grandmother and attending Johnson C. Smith University. One of her tasks in the dorm was to sweep and clean the front steps. She spoke of later being part of the group that implemented the Department of Health, Education and Welfare's Head Start Program.

She was a little country girl who came to the big city of Charlotte and left a global legacy.

When I toured the National Museum of African American History and Culture in 2017, there was an area called The David M. Rubenstein History Galleries: The Journey Toward Freedom. It included a section, "A Changing America: 1968 and Beyond," that referred to the founding of museums and Black Studies programs.

There was the name of Dr. Bertha Maxwell as founder of the program at UNCC. That is a legacy to behold. The epitome of the legacy of a person like Bertha is how she has influenced and shaped a person's endeavors. I know she is proud of all her students' accomplishments.

Ronald S. Swann of Indianapolis is president of the Indianapolis Education Association and chairperson of the Minority Affairs Committee for the Indiana State Teachers Association. He spent decades as a counselor and teacher in public schools and colleges, including Barber-Scotia College, UNCC's Black Studies Department and in the African American Studies Department at Indiana State University. After getting a B.A. in geography in 1971, he earned an M.A. in counseling at UNCC. In 1981, he earned an M.A. in urban economic development at Ohio State University and later completed a teacher-education certification in science.

MODEL OF LEADERSHIP, SISTERHOOD

By Jacqueline Stevens Sanders

I began my college journey at University of North Carolina at Charlotte the fall 1969 as a freshman. This was the semester after students lowered the U.S. flag on campus and demanded a Black Student Union.

For me, this was a frightening and an exciting time. Along with several Black students, I was among the first to live on campus, in Sanford Hall, the first completed dormitory.

My first interaction with Dr. Bertha Maxwell was at a "laboratory retreat" that she organized and that was led by professional consultants Jim Ross, Jim Polk and Jim Burch. During the "Who am I?" exercise, we chose how we identified: colored, Black, Negro, student, etc.

I was the only person who identified as "Negro," which was seen as an outdated and not-cool category by the other students. That experience provided much insight into my experience in a small eastern North Carolina town where I was one of six to integrate the white high school. It was where the Klan had erected a huge welcome sign at the entrance of town.

The retreat was a mind-provoking experience, an element in sharping my future.

I also had a lot of interaction with Dr. Maxwell through chartering the Iota Rho Chapter of Delta Sigma Theta Sorority Inc. on Dec. 13, 1972. It was the first Black Greek-lettered national sorority established on campus. The Charlotte Alumnae Chapter led the initiation process.

Dr. Maxwell helped me, as the chapter president, realize just how good of a leader I am. She helped me to be more confident in my abilities to lead and better interact with others.

The 12 other committed women were Phaedra Berry, Carla Bradley, Vernetta Conley, Charlene Costner, Patricia Hubbard, Claudia Jordan, Maudine McFadden, Cynthia Mullen, Barbara Roseboro, Linda Ross, Marie Todd and Barbara Washington.

We accepted Dr. Maxwell as our mentor and role model. We spent countless hours in her office strategizing and planning car washes, step shows, parties, programs and service projects because we wanted to make an impact on campus life and in the community.

Her profound influence on and support of the "Phenomenal Thirteen" gave true meaning to and provided priceless experiences to evolve a beloved Iota Rho sisterhood.

Dr. Bertha Maxwell Roddey: The light of your great works is apparent to everyone who is blessed to know you. As Psalm 119:105 states, "thy word is a lamp unto my feet, and a light unto my path." I appreciate your leadership and friendship.

Jacqueline Stevens Sanders of Charlotte retired after 39 years as an information-technology project manager with Duke Energy. She earned a B.A. in science in applied mathematics in 1973 and a certificate in project management program in 2007, both from UNCC. Active in the Deltas of Charlotte Foundation and a life member of Jack & Jill of America Inc., she also has held several leadership roles in Grier Heights Presbyterian Church.

CHALLENGE LED TO A MENTOR

By David B. Sanders

I arrived at UNCC for fall semester of 1969, after the taking down of the American flag and the demand for a Black Student Union. Several Black students and I were the first to live in the first dormitories.

Following campus protests, the word was that it was unwise for Black students to walk in groups of more than three.

As I matriculated, I had some interaction with the Black Studies Committee, which was established to create a program focused on the culture, values, contributions, etc., of Black people as it relates to who we are and our contributions in the making of America.

While walking across campus toward the Education Department, a Black woman stopped to speak, and I discovered it was Dr. Bertha Maxwell. Because I knew she would be heading the Black Studies program, I asked her, "What are you going to do for us?"

I was quite passionate in inquiring of her intentions. From that interaction, Dr. Maxwell engaged and galvanized the Black students to start the program.

I worked in the first office with secretary Claudette Cofield. Dr. Maxwell had me write descriptions for the course catalog published by the university, among many other assignments. When I was a graduate student, she gave me a job teaching in the Black Studies program.

She and I formed a powerful mentor-mentee relationship that evolved to a special closeness, even today. Bertha, as she is affectionately known to me, helped me understand how to be confident with who I am and to navigate my way through the world. My teaching style is akin to hers.

David B. Sanders of Charlotte worked more than 30 years in human resources for the City of Charlotte and held national and state positions in related organizations. At UNCC, he earned in B.A in psychology in 1973 and a master of education degree in guidance and counseling in 1977. He has served on the board of the UNCC Black Alumni and was a charter member of the campus Epsilon Zeta chapter of Omega Psi Phi Fraternity. He has received several honors from the fraternity and served in key leadership roles in the Presbyterian Church (USA).

HELPING SHAPE MY DESTINY

By Pamela Hart Winkfield Hemphill

O n my very first day on the campus of the University of North Carolina at Charlotte, while registering for classes, I met Dr. Bertha Maxwell Roddey. She shared with me about the Black Studies Block and the only Black sorority then on campus, Delta Sigma Theta. Her office later became my home away from home as a commuting student. Mother Bertha had an infectious spirit and energy.

I became a very good student and was introduced to so much about self-actualization as a Black female on campus and in the world. She was there as I pledged Delta in April 1976 and, with her as a motivator, I have been financially active ever since.

Always so eager to go to Dr. Roddey's class, I was usually the first in the room. As I waited one day in 1977 for others to come in the classroom, in walked her former student and guest speaker Paul E. Hemphill and his law partner, James Martin.

We talked, and he offered to help me with my civil rights project for the class. I did get an "A" on the project, and from the one who helped me, as well. Several years later, we were married, all because we met in Mother Bertha's classroom.

As Black students on a predominantly white campus, we had great years at UNCC because of Dr. Roddey, secretary Roberta Duff and other Black Studies instructors. We were taught to support each other, to study and be successful as we sought to make a difference in the world.

Motivated by strong Black women like Dr. Bertha Roddey and my mother, Sarah Hart, I became an award-winning teacher, a school administrator, a college instructor and a still-active community servant-leader.

Mother Bertha has been there for her UNCC children, and we have tried to be there for her. She has inspired me to be an overachieving servant-leader. I have loved every assignment.

Pamela Hart Winkfield Hemphill of Charlotte is a professor of English and reading at Central Piedmont Community College. At UNCC, she earned a B.A. in elementary education and teaching in 1979, and a master's of education in reading and elementary education in 1988. In 2000, she received a master's of education in administration with a principal certification from Winthrop University. She worked more than 31 years in Charlotte public schools as an assistant principal, teacher and facilitator. She has been active in political organizations, scholarship programs and religious groups. A charter member of Delta of Charlotte, she has held local, regional and national leadership roles in the sorority, including as chartering advisor for the Davidson College chapter.

SOWING SEEDS OF LEADERSHIP

By Queenie Mackey Byars

I love and appreciate Bertha Maxwell Roddey for her many acts of kindness and look up to her as a role model. She brought genius to UNCC's Black Studies program when our state and country needed it. Bertha demonstrated true grit and great leadership in helping me and countless others.

In high school, I wasn't exposed to the works of notable African-Americans such as James Baldwin, Malcolm X and Harriet Tubman. Bertha's team of inspiring scholars and administrators (Dr. Mary Harper, Dr. Beverly Ford and Roberta Duff) encouraged me to learn more about the African-American diaspora.

When I reflect on the state of race relations and institutional racism in 2020, I'm saddened about the continuing loss of Black lives through racial injustice. We must educate and remind white America that Black Lives Matter — something Bertha taught us.

She sowed the seeds of leadership and stressed the importance of studying Black heritage and civil rights activists. Through history, song, dance, art and poetry, Bertha expanded our cultural appreciation. I remember her support for student activism, the Black Student Union and those who paved the way for me.

One of the most memorable principles in the Black Studies program was assigning student mentors. My upper-class mentors were Vanessa Gallman, Andell McCoy and Marva York. When they transferred to Chapel Hill in 1974, I followed their lead a year later.

Sure, I missed Bertha and my roommate, Debbie Springs, but I wanted to major in journalism, which was not offered at UNCC. At Chapel Hill, I met my soulmate and future husband. Sprouting from Bertha's seeds of leadership, years later I co-directed the Chuck Stone Program for Diversity in Education and Media, a national mentoring program for college-bound students.

I also established the Mackey-Byars Scholarship for Excellence in Communication Excellence for minorities and students with financial need at Chapel Hill — again modeling Bertha.

Queenie Mackey Byars of Efland, N.C., retired in 2014 as an assistant professor at UNC-Chapel Hill, where she taught journalism and public relations. She was honored with a Lifetime Achievement Award from the Raleigh Public Relations Society. She earned her B.A. in journalism from UNC-Chapel Hill in 1977 and a M.A. in communications from the University of Northern Colorado in 1980. During a 20-year Air Force career, she held public affairs assignments in Honduras, Japan and The Pentagon. She retired in 1999 at the rank of lieutenant colonel. She also co-founded a public relations company and served as National Aerospace Awards program manager for the Air Force Association.

IN MEMORIAM

By Artie Lee Travis

W hat tribute would be complete without honoring the accomplishments of those who were touched by Dr. Bertha Maxwell Roddey? Long before my wife of 32 years, Francine Bruce Travis, transitioned to heaven in 2018, Dr. Roddey played an important role in her life.

She was an adviser and big sister to Francine at UNCC. She remained a source of inspiration for Francine though her career in higher and public education. Francine's determination to be great in serving others is one of the tenets taught by Dr. Roddey, a transformational person during a time when transactional was the rule of the day.

Francine — who had three daughters and two granddaughters — was a staunch advocate for and a friend of many other young people. Upon graduating from UNCC and getting a master's from Indiana University, she served as a higher-education administrator for years and later taught nine years as a substitute (while a survivor of cancer) at Rogers Heights Elementary School in Maryland.

Throughout, she developed positive interpersonal relationships with staff members who respected her feedback and sought her advice. She worked as a servant leader at North Carolina State University, Northwestern University in Illinois, the University of Connecticut, Trinity College in the District of Columbia, Greenville Technical College and Spartanburg Methodist College in South Carolina, Agnes Scott College in

Georgia, Elizabeth City State University in North Carolina and the College of Southern Maryland.

Francine's service has been recognized at the elementary school where she taught with the Francine B. Travis Jaguar of the Year Award, a certificate of recognition from the Board of Education in Prince George's County, and a Memorial Resolution from the Maryland Senate.

◊ ◊ ◊

Dr. Artie Lee Travis is vice president for student affairs at Frostburg State University in Maryland.

–Source: Sheryl Westmoreland

Sheryl Westmoreland and Diane Bennett headed to Africa with help from Black Studies program. –Source: Sheryl Westmoreland

Charter members of Iota Rho chapter of Delta Sigma Theta, 1972 –Source: Sheryl Westmoreland

Chilling outside the dining hall –Source: Sheryl Westmoreland

Spencer Singleton and Mary Simpson at 1972 wedding recep-
tion in student center –Source: Spencer Singleton

Bonnie Cone and Bertha Maxwell, both retired, at 1992 din-
ner honoring Kappa Alpha Psi –Source: Spencer Singleton

Students in first Black Studies Block in 1972 –Source: Terry Smith

Students in first Black Studies Block in 1972 Source: Terry Smith

View of main campus in early 1970s –Source: Terry Smith

Getting an autograph from "Roots" author
Alex Haley –Source: Terry Smith

–Source: Kevin T. King

Students taking a break on the Belk Bell Tower
in late 1970s –Source: Robert Rowell

Alpha Phi Alpha step show in late 1970s –Source: Robert Rowell

Ronald Swann jokes with Bertha Maxwell during a 1977
Black Studies awards dinner –Source: Ronald Swann

Children of the Sun gospel choir prepares to perform during
International Festival –Source: Debbie Woodson

Dr. Beverly Ford, psychology professor in
Black Studies –Source: Avis Wilson

First line for Alpha Kappa Alpha chapter in 1975 –Source: Annette Pearce

Black Student

Union

Founding members of Black Student Union, officially recognized on Nov. 26, 1969 –Source: DigitalNC.org

Annette Johnson, left, and Emma Gillespie on 1973-74 cheerleading team –Source: DigitalNC.org

Kappa Alpha Psi in the 1970 yearbook –Source: DigitalNC.org

Linda Ross as "Miss 49'er" in 1972 –Source: DigitalNC.org

Cora Pearson as Homecoming Queen in 1972 –Source: DigitalNC.org

Omega Psi Phi in the 1973 yearbook –Source: DigitalNC.org

Students' 1969 Ten Demands –Source: DigitalNC.org

SECTION IV

AFTERWORD

STUDENT PROTEST: PAST
IS PROLOGUE

By Herman E. Thomas

T he Black Studies program at the University of North Carolina
at Charlotte intentionally pursued departmental status to
obtain and assure academic respect and validity.

Why? Because Black lives mattered.

The task was challenging, but the results could be revolutionary.
We could move from segregation to completeness, the fulfillment
of the ideals ensconced in the Declaration of Independence and
the Constitution.

Yet the prime focus was — and had to be — the student.
Students initiated the protests and marches; they placed their academic pursuits in the crosshairs of struggle and opposition.

I understood that commitment. A passion for initiating change
and progress had been engrained in my being long before my
arrival at UNCC.

I was directly involved in the student sit-ins at the Woolworth's lunch counter that began Feb. 1, 1960, in Greensboro. I still have visions of crossing under the Market Street Bridge marching to the store. Several of the Greensboro Four — including Franklin McCain, who would later be my roommate and lifelong friend — lived near me in Scott Hall at North Carolina A&T State University.

For several consecutive days, I was a regular sit-in demonstrator. Then I became an organizer behind the scenes, securing class notes and course information for those sitting at the counters, and providing personal items such as toiletries and blankets for those arrested.

Social action felt natural to me. Yet I was not considered a good candidate for arrest because of my family's leadership in one of the earliest attempts in North Carolina to desegregate a public school.

In 1956, I sought to desegregate Swain County's only high school, which was three miles from my home. Jackson County Colored High School was a 44-mile roundtrip. Our efforts were unsuccessful. But rather than attend an all-Black high school with fewer than 20 students, I sought out the best schools in nearby states. That meant attending three different high schools: in Ohio, Tennessee and North Carolina.

That's why, to this day, I do not and will not tolerate mediocrity when excellence is possible, the classroom and demonstrations not excepted.

When I worked for Springfield College in Massachusetts, efforts to establish a Black Studies Department, which I would chair, were hastened when Black and white students united in building "takeovers." But in spring 1974, the South and UNCC — where students, faculty, staff and community converged — beckoned.

The perspectives of the students' "10 Demands" simplified into four questions: "Who am I? Where did I come from? Where am I going? Where do I go from here?" These four questions informed development of the four phases of the Black Studies curriculum.

I was coordinator of the final phase, which required completion of a bound and preserved project that was the equivalent of an undergraduate thesis. It had to be presented and defended before a committee of faculty, students and community representatives.

Students were required to utilize research standards of the discipline of their major and the research standards of African-American and African Studies. This interdisciplinary approach could lead to clarification and refinement of the non-African-American methodology, and culminate in improved understanding and the potential for wider application.

The freedom to explore the African-American experience opened new avenues of thought and provided self-respect and self-affirmation. These studies intentionally entwined the individual with community, as expressed in the African dictum: "I am because we are, and since we are, therefore I am."

That sentiment is the crux of the past and impels us on the present trajectory to self- and communal affirmation. How interesting that Black Studies emerged from students seeking self-actualization through higher education at a mostly white campus.

By the mid-1980s, the Black Studies Block (several courses that required enrollment in Black Studies courses, as well as other classes) had an institutional format and campus respectability. That initiative then fostered creation of the University Transition Opportunities Program (UTOP), a summer program focused on recruitment, retention and graduation.

Incoming freshmen earned seven credit hours during the five-week session; many later registered for The Block courses. UTOP began in 1986 with 16 students; in 2019, it enrolled more than 100 African-American, Hispanic, white and Native American students. A 2011 national survey listed UTOP among the nation's top 11 summer transition programs.

Black lives matter. They always have. Black Studies, African-American Studies, Africana Studies and UTOP matter. They always will.

Today is but prologue to the future. Let the spirit of the ancestors shine within and upon us all.

◊ ◊ ◊

The Rev. Dr. Herman E. Thomas of Charlotte is former assistant director of UNCC's Black Studies program, emeritus professor of religious studies and founder/coordinator of the University Transition Opportunities Program. A retired vice president of academic affairs at Shaw University, he holds degrees from North Carolina A&T State University, Duke University Divinity School and Hartford Seminary Foundation. He currently serves as senior associate pastor at First Baptist Church West.

UNCC students' March Against Injustice, June 2020. Source: UNCC